RUST HILLS SAYS:

"If you want to know how short stories work, then I think I can help you . . . I've been messing around with other people's fiction for so long—working on short stories and novel sections and getting them into magazines, tinkering with work by established writers and trying to bring work by new writers into focus—and I've been *thinking* so much over all these years, and I've compiled so many anthologies of contemporary American fiction, and I've been reading and checking out what I thought against those anthologies of yours, and *talking* with so many writers and ruining my life with this *book* for so long—that I really do think I know something about it now."

writing in general and the short story in particular

An Informal Textbook

by Rust Hills

BANTAM BOOKS
TORONTO · NEW YORK · LONDON · SYDNEY

This low-priced Bantam Book
has been completely reset in a type face
designed for easy reading, and was printed
from new plates. It contains the complete
text of the original hard-cover edition.
NOT ONE WORD HAS BEEN OMITTED.

RL 8, IL 9-up

WRITING IN GENERAL AND
THE SHORT STORY IN PARTICULAR

*A Bantam Book / published by arrangement with
Houghton Mifflin Company*

PRINTING HISTORY

*Houghton Mifflin edition published November 1977
Serialized in* THE WRITER *April 1978*
Bantam edition / January 1979
2nd printing .... September 1980

ISBN 0–553–14576–2

Published simultaneously in the United States and Canada

11 10 9 8 7 6 5 4 3

Contents

Introduction

I've got a shelf of how-to-write books, and they all seem to me pretty much dreadful, especially the ones about the short story. They all seem to be written by old magazine hacks about a kind of "popular" formula fiction no one wants anymore anyway—*Story Plotting Simplified*, that kind of thing, complete with simple-minded examples from slick fiction.

Then I've got another shelf of books, some of them seem to me great. These are college textbook anthologies of short stories, with analyses of the stories that sometimes get quite technical. Basically these are how-to-read books, like Mark Schorer's *The Story: A Critical Anthology*. But it seems to me that a beginning writer could learn more from any one of them—from, say, just the "Glossary of Technical Terms" at the back of Cleanth Brooks and Robert Penn Warren's *Understanding Fiction*—than he ever could from reading the whole damn *shelf* of the how-to-write ones.

The difference of course is that the first shelf is trying to teach you how to write lousy stories, and the second shelf is trying to teach you how to read literature. But who wants to write lousy stories anyway? What young writers want to write, or ought to want to write, is literature. Is it absurd to think of, a how-to-write book about the literary short story?

Well, yes, I guess it is, sort of. But there's all those writing *courses* out there, at the colleges and universities; and the young-poet English teachers and the writers-in-residence there aren't trying to teach "boy meets girl" and "know your market." They're trying to teach their kids to write short story masterpieces, like the ones they study in the anthologies. It's a hopeless job, of course, 99 percent of the time, or more—but what harm could a book do, trying to do the same hopeless thing?

Besides, I think maybe this book could possibly help some of those famous writers-in-residence. Say a kid comes to famous writer and says, in that arrogant but not really off-putting way good young kids sometimes have, "Teach me to write great short stories." So maybe the famous writer-in-residence could now laugh and say, "Yes, well, okay, but first go read Rust Hills' book for the basics—for the essential techniques of fiction and how they function—and then come back to me and I'll teach you what I know." Also, I imagine that this book might help some person who's off by himself somewhere, if there's anyone left like that, to learn to read literary stories in such a way as to help him to write them.

I've been working on this book for twenty years, off and on, mostly off. It began when I was working at *Esquire* as Fiction Editor. I took the slick fiction out of *Esquire* and converted the magazine over to literary fiction. I really did that. I published most of the major writers of our time. They were all amazed, at least at first. Later I tried to do the same at *The Saturday Evening Post* and it didn't work so well—not at all so well. After that I was hired to publish literary fiction from the very beginning at a hardcover magazine called *Audience,* but it didn't last long. I know something about what's hopeless.

When I was at *Esquire* I tried teaching short story writing at Columbia, N.Y.U., and The New School. This was in their adult extension programs, one night a week, and talk about your hopeless. Terrible abrupt nurses and retired accountants who thought they had a tale to tell, and I got to dreading Wednesday nights when they'd get together and quarrel with one another and not understand anything I said. Let me admit it right now: what I have to say about short stories in this book won't help you a bit if you are a terrible abrupt nurse or a retired accountant with a tale to tell.

There has got to be a minimum basic kind of competence before you can even begin to *think* of writing, and there's got to be a whole hell of a lot more than that before you can even dream about being one of those writers who appear in the how-to-read anthologies. It can happen. You don't have to be a better person. You just have to have a peculiar slice-of-the-mind that sees and says things in a peculiar and accurate way—that's all, just an originality of perception and utterance.

But granted that, if you want to know how short stories work, what the particular dynamics of that kind of fiction which is the Modernist (*not* the "New Fiction") short story are—if you want to know that, then I think maybe I can help you. I really do. I'm amazed at it myself. But I've been messing around with other people's fiction for so long—working on short stories and novel sections and getting them into magazines, tinkering with work by established writers and trying to bring work by new writers into focus—and I've been *thinking* about it so much over all these years, and I've compiled so many anthologies of contemporary American fiction, and I've been reading and checking out what I thought against those anthology masterpieces of yours, and *talking* with so many writers, and ruining my life with this *book* for so long—that I really do think I know something about it now.

All *you* have to have is originality of perception and utterance; and if you've really got that, you're the kind of person who could really use this book without really probably needing it in the first place, if you see what I mean.

R.H.

writing in general and
the short story in particular

The Short Story, as against the Novel and the Sketch

This book implies that some techniques of fiction tend to have absolute effects, and tries to explain what they are.

As far as the short story itself is concerned, I won't even attempt a definition. Everyone knows what a short story is anyway—whether it be a prose narrative glibly described as "shorter than a novel" or as the first commentator on the form, Edgar Allan Poe, specified, "no longer than can be read in a single sitting." And I'm taking for granted the distinction between the literary short story and what used to be called the "slick" story—both the soupy, romantic fiction once found in ladies' magazines and the adventury, fantasying, apparently-hard-boiled-but-at-bottom-sentimental stories of sports or crime or outdoor life that passed as "man's" fiction. My distinction, then, is prose narrative of a certain quality as well as not beyond a certain length.

Beyond that, I believe that only two things can be said about the nature of the short story, and these statements seem at first so different from each other and so unrelated as to appear random. First, a short story tells of something that happened to someone. Second, the successful contemporary short story will demonstrate a more harmonious relationship of all its aspects than will any other literary art form, excepting perhaps lyric poetry. In fact, these two statements *are* quite a lot to say. The first statement distinguishes the story from the sketch, the second distinguishes it from the novel.

A short story is different from a sketch because "a short story tells of something that happened to somebody." A sketch is by definition a static description of a character or a place or whatever. In character sketches, the character described remains constant. If there is passage of time in a character sketch—for instance, if we are shown the sequence of the character's day, from mornng until night—the character is assumed to be the same each morning, each noon, each night. If there is action or episode, it is used merely to illustrate the character's character, not to develop it; he learns nothing from it, changes not a whit. Any incident in a sketch is rendered as an *example* of a character's behavior, not as the account of something that happened to him that moved or altered him, as it is in a story. It's assumed that confronted with the same situation on another occasion, the character in a sketch would react in exactly the same way again, no matter how many times the action was repeated.

A story, however, is dynamic rather than static: the same thing *cannot* happen again. A character is capable of being moved, and *is* moved, no matter in how slight a way.

The novel differs from the short story in more than just length, but they both share this quality of character-moved-by-plot. But the difference is, that on the long trip the novel provides, there is space/time for a quantity of incidents and effects. Edgar Allan Poe spoke of the short story as providing "a single and unique effect" toward which every word contributes: "If his [the author's] very initial sentence tend not to the outbringing of this effect, then he has failed in his first step. In the whole composition there should be no word written, of which the tendency, direct or indirect, is not to the one pre-established design." Poe's famous "unique effect" dictum can of course be taken too strictly, but it does seem to be the case that there is a degree of unity in a well-wrought story—what we have called an "harmonious relationship of all its aspects"—that isn't necessarily found in a good novel, that isn't perhaps even desirable in a novel.

Each aspect of fiction technique—characterization, plot, point of view, theme, style or language, setting, symbol or imagery; "divide" them as you will—will be used in subtly different fashion by the short story writer and the novelist, though the same man be the one one morning and the other the next. The story writer will not usually elaborate secondary characters, won't usually mess much with subplots. Where the novelist may bounce around in point of view, shifting the angle of narration from one character to another, to focus first here, then there, the short story writer will usually maintain a single point of view, so as to keep the whole of his story in focus.

The story writer won't use any of the aspects of fiction technique loosely, the way a novelist may. In a story everything's bound together tightly. The theme in a successful story is inseparably embedded in the action taken by the characters—and indeed is implicit in all the other aspects, even the language. In density of language, in multiple use of the sound and sense of words, the short story is comparable to lyric poetry. Eudora Welty's short story "Livvie" has a complex and intricate system of imagery, from fable, myth, and fairy tale, that reminds one of Eliot or Pound. Hemingway's "A Clean, Well-Lighted Place" has sustained poetic metaphor, on death and light and sex, that recalls a Shakespeare sonnet or a Donne lyric. Even so long a story as Henry James' "The Turn of the Screw" can be read as a poem; for the richness of phrase and symbol elaborating the angelic-diabolic conflict, although it may go all-but-unnoticed by a reader caught in the grip of the story, enhances the aura and meaning marvelously.

In the short story, language has a multitude of other roles, beyond simply achieving the narration. For instance, in any description of the setting—and the setting, whether it be lonely room or crowded city, will be chosen carefully for its connections with the theme as well as the action—the language (enhanced by symbol and imagery) will have the theme implicit in it. And language will also create *style*, will imply the author's *tone*, will be used for *atmosphere* or *mood*, may be a foreshadowing device of the *plot*, will certainly depend on the *point of view* from which the story is told (for language and style and tone are entirely interdependent with the angle of narration, the point of view chosen), and may contribute to the *characterization* of the point-of-view figure.

A successful short story will thus necessarily show a more harmonious relationship of part to whole, and part to part, than it is usual ever to find in a novel. Everything must work with everything else. Everything enhances everything else, interrelates with everything else, is inseparable from everything else—and all this is done with a necessary and perfect economy.

Character and Action

> I shall be telling this with a sigh
> Somewhere ages and ages hence:
> Two roads diverged in a wood, and I—
> I took the one less traveled by,
> And that has made all the difference.
>
> Robert Frost
> "The Road Not Taken"

Nothing can happen again. If we accept the non-uncommon metaphor implied in Frost's poem that Life is a journey, then the road not taken can never be taken. Confronted with a choice that seems important to him, a person may use the outright cliché: "My life's at a crossroads." But the fork in the road is more diagramatically accurate of what he's faced with. A man often finds himself in a situation where he feels he must "go one way or the other." Sometimes he seems to have a choice of which way to go; sometimes he feels he has no choice, but is "pushed into it." Other times he may not even be aware that he's taken one path instead of another, but just "Follows his nose," blindly.

In any event, there is only one road a person can take, only one way anyone can ever be. How much choice he ever had is a matter for the philosophers and psychologists who debate about free will versus various sorts of determinism. If we are all being pushed around by an omnipotent omniscient God or by psychologically predetermined behavior patterns or by mechanistic socioeconomic forces—if so, we are not much aware of it. Perhaps our lives are analogous to those of characters in fiction whose nature and fate is in the hands of an author. In fiction, an author sets a character out on the road in the first place and then within certain limitations, shoves him down whatever paths the author wants him to take for as long as he wants him to go.

But the author is ultimately responsible to the reader, although this responsibility is often denied. The author must explain to the reader why a character took one road instead of the other—must explain or show by the action of the plot why the character chose a particular road or how he was forced into it by circumstances or other characters—and the author must make clear that it was a significantly different road.

In every short story a fork in the road is encountered. The author can show the character taking a new road or show him passing it by. In either case "something has happened to someone." As a result of the action of the story—as a result of what "happens" in the story—a way that the character could have taken, a way he could have been, is no longer possible for him. Or his life has taken a new direction, however slight the change may be.

Fate is as irreversible in fiction as it is in life. The author may use various methods to make it seem to the reader that the character has choice, has a chance to be other than he will be, has opportunity to do other than he does. The reader submits to these methods, first of all because they delight him, but also because he in turn has a hold over the author: whatever finally happens must be convincing. That is, in retrospect every turn of the action must seem inevitable.

"Character is Fate," said Heraclitus in 500 B.C. or

thereabouts. But "Our characters are the result of our conduct," added Aristotle, a hundred years or so later. We will find character and action even more inseparably entwined in fiction than they appear to be in life.

Fixed Action, as against Moving Action

It is an effective way of achieving characterization in fiction to show how a character regularly behaves, what his actions are in his everyday life. Every action he takes—from how he brushes his teeth in the morning to how he winds his alarm clock as he goes to bed at night—all such actions indicate, or are capable of indicating, something significant about him. And "little" habits (like what's carried in pockets) may be as revealing as the "big" things (like the attitude assumed when talking with the boss). These are "fixed actions." People are doing things all the time, but in the same way every time. The key thing about these actions is that they are repeated—indeed, the fact that they are done over and over is what makes them significant and revealing.

There is a kind of larger pattern of behavior that people fall into too; not just the day-to-day routine, but a sort of repetitious pattern to their whole lives. Some of these life patterns are very bizarre. Troubled people try all sorts of ways to solve their problems and sometimes adopt a role or manner that ought to be temporary or transitional, but then they get stuck that way. It's like when the needle gets stuck in one groove of the Victrola record: there's still sound and there's still movement; but the sound is senseless and the movement is somehow static, going around in circles.

People get stuck, for instance, playing the role of either parent or child in situations where all that's wanted is to be simply adult. They make their rounds, daily, yearly, seeking a particular kind of kick or caress that they've been stuck into wanting. As often as not they keep going to those who can't possibly give them what they want. Or if it's what they want, they shouldn't want it. Everyone knows how everyone else ought to live his life. Many patterns of life are almost incredibly self-destructive, but nonetheless familiar. There's the man who constantly takes on more than he can manage so that he can fail, doomed in some psychologically predetermined way to want the failure that he hates. There's the familiar Don Juan figure—now a stereotype in both literature and psychology—doomed to go from girl to girl but never to find the "lasting relationship" he says he seeks. There's the accident-prone person; the hard-luck person. We all notice how much the ex-wives of a much-married man resemble the girl he's marrying now. Some women seem only to choose alcoholics for husbands, over and over. Poor people! With new enthusiasm and firm resolve to break out of their maze, they waste their vitality by inevitably rushing into the same corridor as before, to make the choice that puts them right back where they were.

Not all patterned behavior is so extreme or so self-destructive. There are of course tendencies toward repetitious behavior in every life: many apparently happy and profitable lives are built around routine and repetition. We've all recognized patterned, predictable behavior in our acquaintances. It's harder to see it in ourselves, but pattern in action, whether in daily habits or in entire existence, is likely to be the rule rather than the exception.

But just the opposite is true in fiction. In fiction this kind of "fixed action" is an aspect of characterization rather than plot. Patterned behavior is useful in establishing characterization because it is illustrative action that shows what a character is like. The very fact that these sequences of action happen over and over is especially revealing of character. But it is distinctly different from the action which comprises the plot of a short story. What happens in a short story can happen only once. A short story may show how a character got his needle stuck and got into one of these patterns of circular, "static," fixed movement. Or a story may show the extraordinary and exceptional circumstances by which a character broke out or was jolted out of the groove he was stuck in. In some rare cases a story may show how a character lost his last chance to get out. But in any event, the action in fiction is not this static action, friezed in constant motion like the figures going around and around the urn but getting nowhere. Such patterns of behavior are described at the beginning of a story to create characterization. Or they are suggested at the end of a story as the result of the action, as showing what the character became as a result of what happened to him in the story.

But the action in fiction is final determining action. Something happens, however slight it may be—and it isn't something that happened over and over before and is going to happen again and again in the future. It is assumed that the events of a story take place only once, that whatever "happens" to the character as a result of the action of the story alters or "moves" him in such a way, again however slight it may be, that he would never experience or do the same thing in exactly the same way. Moving action alters fixed action.

As the Story Begins and Ends

Martin lived alone in a two-room apartment on the East Side. It was his habit every morning, after arising and shaving and bathing, and dressing, to plug in his electric coffee percolator, and while it was perking, go downstairs to his mailbox, get his mail and his newspaper, and go back upstairs and read them while he was having breakfast.

But one morning when he went down to the mailbox . . .

The first paragraph describes action Martin takes, but it is "fixed action," taken in the same way each time, a pattern of regular behavior that exemplifies his way of life and to some extent helps establish his situation and his characterization. The second paragraph introduces a potential story. Whatever happens to Martin as a result of his visit to the mailbox that particular morning—whether he encounters the seemingly nice girl in the next apartment just coming in at that hour, or whether he gets a letter saying a lesbian CIA agent has murdered his uncle in Beirut—whatever he does as a result, whatever happens to him as a result, is not an action that could be repeated every day. Nor is it the kind of action that could ever be repeated in exactly the same way. The first paragraph describes action that is understood to be fixed—that is, constant (or repeatable) before the story happens, for it may be that afterward, as a result of the specific action introduced this particular morning at the mailbox, afterward his regular morning habits may be quite different.

> Martin had always had a lot of girls, but when-
> ever one of them seemed to be getting too involved
> with him he'd back off and find a new one.
> But one night at a party he met Jane . . .

It should be understood that these first paragraphs are putting matters oversuccinctly. It might be the author's desire to show at some length the regular pattern of Martin's relations with girls. He could describe in some detail, perhaps even dramatize into scenes, his experiences with Betty and Sue and Genevieve and the nice girl next door and so on *as a preamble to the story*. It's assumed that whatever happened with Betty and Sue and all the others followed the pattern of action described. But what happens with Jane, if it is a story, will be unique. It will not be the sort of action which could take place over and over, because Martin will have been affected by the action of the story and could not again go through the same experience with

Jane in exactly the same way. No matter what he did to her or she to him, it could not happen again.

Of course, nothing can happen again. And of course what happened with Genevieve really must have had some effect on Martin and couldn't have happened again either. But that's not the story. Every day that passes affects Martin somewhat and he can't even go down to the mailbox exactly the same way twice in a row. But a story assumes a constant to start with. A story has to begin somewhere, and, as it begins, there is so to speak a split instant of pause when we see Martin as he is "now"—now as the story begins. This is when the author sets him out on the road. And the story tells of what happened to him from that point on to some other pont which is the end. At the end there is another split instant of pause when we see what has happened to him as a result of the action of the story. Then he simply vanishes just as he simply appeared at the beginning—according to the author's will.

The character to whom the events of the story have consequence is a *moved* character. There may, of course, be several moved characters in a novel, but in the short story there is usually just one character on whom matters focus. He is "moved" in the sense that at the end of the story he is not in exactly the same place he was at the beginning. He has been affected, "changed," is somehow different—no matter in how slight a way. It may be a very slight movement indeed—a change barely suggested by the author, amounting perhaps to little more then just a shift in the author's tone, the altering effect of a symbol or image. But something has happened. The character has *moved*, emotionally. He must be presented as a *dynamic* (moving or movable) character, rather than as a *static* (stationary) character, in order for him to do this.

Loss of the Last Chance to Change

It might be well to mention here a kind of story that seems at first to be a character sketch. At the end a character appears unaltered, may seem in fact deeper in his groove than ever. And yet there may be a feeling that something really has in fact happened to him. Often such a story will be based on the semicliché of "loss of last chance to change." Martin, now in late middle-age, yearns to get married and alter his described regular lonely existence. In the past he has met girls, but always been too shy and retiring to press his suit (clichés often lead to ambiguities this way). *In the course of the story* he meets another girl, better than all the others and more available to him (she doesn't care if his suit is pressed), but again he fails. The reader is to understand as the story ends that Martin has lost his last chance to change and will now stay "forever" as he was. But of course he is not the same at the end of the story as he was at the beginning: he has altered, for that which was there before—the capacity for change—has been removed from his character and circumstances by the action of the story. What's different at the end is that there's no longer any possibility for him to become otherwise than he is; that's what "happened" to him.

Recognizing the Crucial

At some point in the creation of his story it is probably necessary, and certainly at least useful, for a writer to have a general overall sense of what it is that happens to his character as a result of the action, how the action changed him, when exactly it happened, and so forth. This awareness of what he's doing can be present before he even begins writing, or when he starts to revise the first draft (probably the best time), or even when he's reading the story over in the magazine that published it—at some point he ought to be aware of what he's doing.

A good exercise for beginning writers, to make them aware of how incident does alter character, is to describe in some detail an older person they know fairly well. The exercise is to analyze the person's general situation and personality and pattern of life—roughly, in ways that are psychological or sociological rather than "literary"—and then try to figure out, or even just guess, how the older person came to be that way, what happened to him that made him that way. It is necessary to imagine back to an earlier time when the "subject" might have been different, when he was capable of becoming some other way than the way he is now—and then provide an incident that took him past the other possibilities. Take an aunt or uncle, for instance:

> My Uncle Martin is a cynical sort of man, who nevertheless seems to enjoy his life. He is a bachelor who has never married and he has a good time joking with all the widows who live around here. He's nice to them and cheers them up and all, but sometimes he seems to take advantage of them. (Mother says they sometimes pay the bill when he takes them out to dinner.) He often comes to din-

ner at our house, and I think he is somewhat lonely.

As to how he came to be this way, my mother once told me about Uncle Martin and some friend of my mother's named Jane. It seems that . . .

or:

My Aunt Genevieve is the only one of my relatives I can't stand. She is always angry and mean and yelling about something. If I were one of her kids I'd move out, and they will soon too. The way she bosses my Uncle Walt around is terrible, and he is a nice guy, although I have to admit he's not good looking or much of a success in business or anything. Dad once told me that Aunt Gen married on the rebound and that disappointment in love had soured her on life. There was apparently only one man in her life, ever, and he treated her very bady and hardly even realized it. She was very beautiful when she was young and she worked in New York a year and was very happy and in love with this young lawyer named Martin. But then one day . . .

In trying to track back to the moment when their aunts and uncles first started to become the way they are now, these nieces and nephews seek to isolate a particular episode or sequence of episodes that is crucial, to locate that fork in the road that "ages hence" (in the words of Frost's poem) "has made all the difference." The theory of the exercise is that recognizing a truly crucial episode in life will help the writer to construct a really true crisis in fiction.

Of course what happens in life isn't just due to taking one big fork in the road instead of another; it is due to a series of small choices and small pressures that cumulatively determine personality and situation, which in turn causes choices and pressures—a constant interaction between behavior and personality and circumstance that eventually becomes your life history. But not every event, even in real life, is equally important.

A short story writer seeks to isolate those events that are most significant and then focus on them. The sequences that are most important he'll render in detail, dramatizing them in scenes so as to bring them to life. What "happens" to a character may happen over a series of incidents, but there is likely to be one of those incidents that can be regarded as central or crucial: the point at which, or *after which,* there is no turning back; a climactic moment when all the other possible ways the character could go became significantly less possible.

Naming the Moment

There are a great many words and terms that are used to refer to this incident or moment in the story. Four that seem especially useful are "crisis," "critical moment," "climax," and "crucial moment." These words may all seem pretty much alike, but their origins suggest different shadings in their meaning. "Crisis" is from the Greek *krisis,* meaning "to separate." "Critical" is from the greek *kritikos,* meaning "able to judge." "Climax" is from the Greek *klimax,* meaning "ladder." And "crucial" is from the Latin *crux,* meaning "cross."

The word we want for this moment in fiction would partake of all four of these words, their derivations, and more. It would reflect both a general crucial (trying, severe) period and a critical (decisive, of doubtful issue) situation on the one hand, and a particular crucial (final and supreme) and climactic (culminating, ultimate) moment on the other. It would partake of the ladder image, for there is often a series of crises before a final climax which is crucial—the idea of an "ascending action." The ideal term would reflect the idea of separating: separating the past from the future by this incident, and indicating that the moment comprises a sort of watershed from which the river of the character's life runs one way or

14

the other. The ideal word would reflect the idea of judgment, too; for somewhere in the story, in the author's tone, in the character's motivation, in the ironies implicit in the situation—somewhere there would be a sense of the validity or appropriateness of the judgment rendered the character by the action. And the cross image is relevant too—not just in the sense of a life at a crossroads—but in the sense of a supreme trial.

The ideal term would suggest too that the moment is "dynamic," effecting alteration or movement in character, in plot, and in the whole story in various ways. Like "central moment" the ideal term would indicate that it is to this point that a story moves and from it that it falls away. Like "dènouement" or "recognition scene" or "moment of revelation," it would suggest that at this point in the story something more of the situation is made apparent or clear, to the reader, perhaps, as well as to the character, and that as a result the character may learn something about himself and others, have a "moment of truth." Like "key moment" the term would suggest mysteries unlocked and discoveries made, and suggest that the scene or episode in question is the keystone that supports the whole arch of the story, Like "moment of reversal" it would suggest a turnabout from the way the story has gone so far to some other way. Like "turning point" the ideal term would suggest the still center of the wheel of action, the point the whole story centers on, turns on.

"Epiphany" as a Literary Term

There are many other terms too, besides all these, and perhaps anyway they don't all refer to the same thing. A good deal of the trouble with a lot of the terms in which short stories are discussed is that they come to us originally from drama theory or from the formulas of slick fiction. One term, however, that we have not hitherto mentioned is particularly appropriate to the modern short story and its subtle effects. It is "epiphany," a word that James Joyce used in special, but confusing ways.

Epiphany-with-a-capital-E refers now to the twelfth day after Christmas; its eve is Twelfth Night. Twelve days after Jesus was born in Bethlehem, the Magi (the three wise men) saw Him there: He was manifested or shown to them as king of the Gentiles. The feast or festival of the Epiphany also commemorates two other events in the life of Christ: his baptism by John, when his sonship to God was made manifest to the world; and the miracle at Cana, when he turned water to wine at a wedding and first manifested his divine powers. The word is from the Greek *epiphaneia*, meaning "appearance," derived from *epi*, meaning "to," plus *phaineim*, meaning "show." Thus: "to show to." And "epiphany"—now without a capital E—means any such luminous, divine manifestation. De Quincey, for instance, spoke of the "epiphanies of the Greek intellect."

The Joycean concept of the epiphany is even more secular. In 1900, when James Joyce was eighteen or thereabouts, he had not had much luck publishing his poetry, so he started writing carefully wrought little pieces of nonpoetry, which he called "epiphanies." *Stephen Hero*, the manuscript of Joyce's discarded version of the autobiographical novel of his youth in Dublin that was entirely rewritten as *Portrait of the Artist as a Young Man*, describes how Joyce may have begun to record his epiphanies. Stephen, who is for the most part the young James Joyce, "was passing through Eccles' St one evening, one misty evening . . ." when he heard a "fragment of colloquy" between a young lady and a young gentleman "out of which he received an impression keen enough to afflict his sensitiveness very severely."

The fragment is recorded, then, as Joyce writes of Stephen:

This triviality made him think of collecting many such moments together into a book of epiphanies. By an epiphany he meant a sudden spiritual manifestation, whether in the vulgarity of speech or of gesture or in a memorable phase of the mind itself. He believed it was for the man of letters to record these epiphanies with extreme care, seeing that they themselves are the most delicate and evanescent of moments.

There are forty of Joyce's epiphanies that survive in manuscript, although he has numbered them as high as seventy-one, and there were obviously more. Some of them were worked in as material for *Stephen Hero* or *Portrait of the Artist as a Young Man,* and some are not.

One reason for the confusion about Joyce's use of the word is that his epiphanies are both a kind of experience and also a literary genre—both a way of seeing or hearing and also a way of showing and writing. And within the genre of his epiphanies there are several confusingly different sorts of them. Some are fragments of overheard conversations of strangers; some are accounts of dreams; some are brief dialogues between Joyce and persons he knew; some are entirely uncategorizable. The matter is complicated by the fact that some of the epiphanies seem to be artistic creation—in fact, a sort of poetic-prose statement—while others seem simply to be transcriptions of actual life, although recorded, of course, "with extreme care." If the epiphany is in fact a literary genre invented by Joyce, then it is impossible to define or describe the nature of the form. Often the form epiphanies seem most to resemble is what we may call "the well-worked entry in the writer's notebook."

But epiphany is used in another way by Joyce, in connection with the theory of aesthetics presented by Stephen. Stephen translates Acquinas' *claritas* as "radiance" and defines it as the "luminous silent stasis of esthetic pleasure," distinguishing it from the kinetic response evoked by improper arts, such as those which are didactic or pornographic. *Claritas*, says Stephen, is *quidditas*, "the whatness of a thing."

> This is the moment which I call epiphany . . . when the relation of the parts [of an art object] is exquisite . . . its soul, its whatness leaps to us from the vestment of its appearance. The soul of the commonest object, the structure of which is so adjusted, seems to us radiant. The object achieves its epiphany.

But beyond the genre and aesthetic-theory aspects of the Joycean epiphany are implications about literary method. There is an understated, uninsistent quality to the writing that is very familiar to us now, but must have seemed very distinctive when first used. As Richard Ellmann says in his biography, Joyce "cradles" in his epiphanies "the technique which has now become a commonplace of modern fiction." Ellmann continues:

> Arrogant yet humble too, it claims importance by claiming nothing; it seeks a presentation so sharp that comment by the author would be an interference . . . The author abandons himself and the reader to his material.

The method, as used by Joyce, is really best seen in the short stories collected in *Dubliners,* which he wrote at the same time he was drafting *Stephen Hero.* Although none of his extant epiphanies are to be found transferred into these stories, many of the short stories can be considered to be extended, developed, sustained epiphanies in themselves. The implications of what's so carefully described in these stories is never made explicitly clear by the author; the effect of them seems to fade off into a quiet, a silence—"the luminous silent stasis" of the epiphany.

The epiphany (whether considered as a technique or an effect or a theory or a genre) is a much more useful concept for the short story than it is for the novel. Even Joyce himself could not seem to make it work in a novel. He had originally intended to collect a small book of his epiphanies, but he later thought that he could work them into the manuscript of the

"EPIPHANY" AS A LITERARY TERM

novel *Stephen Hero*. This is admittedly not a finished work—the first 400-odd pages of the manuscript are missing, and Joyce had intended to destroy the whole—but it is a very readable book and somehow more open and revealing than *Portrait*. But it is very flawed as a work of art, perhaps because the little epiphanies, each with its own stasis, keep interrupting the flow of the book. After each of the epiphanies in *Stephen Hero*, Joyce has to crank up and get the narrative moving all over again. The epiphanies are used much more sparingly in *Portrait* and more successfully, notably in the high-flying passage at the very end of the book.

But in many modern short stories since Joyce, the whole effect and meaning may resemble the effect and unstated meaning of an epiphany. The "movement" of character by action that we have been speaking of may not represent an alteration so much as it does a further manifestation. It is something like this that is meant by the teacher of writing when he says to the student of writing about the ending of a fine story they have been "appreciating" together: "Yes, there is an epiphany." He means that as a result of what happens in the story, something—the "whatness" of a character or of a situation—has been made manifest, has been shown forth, has shone forth.

It is probably wrong to go on, as many who use the word do, to refer to a certain passage as being "the" epiphany of a story, or to refer to a character "having" an epiphany. "Yes," says the instructor, "it is clear that at the end of the story Martin has an epiphany." By this he means, most likely, that the central figure has some sort of revelation, something or other is made manifest to him: in a little thought-balloon over his head, a light bulb goes on. Yet why should not the word be used in these ways too, if it serves a purpose? The meaning of "epiphany" has always been elastic—why not stretch if further? We have no other word or term that conveys so many of the subtle effects of this technique of fiction.

The Inevitability of Retrospect

The action of a story, then, takes a character past a decisive point down into one or another of the forks in the road. As a result of "what happens" there is one chance less that he can become anything other than what it is inevitable he will become. When the story is over there is one opportunity less among the opportunities that seemed to be there for him to go any other way than the way he is fated to go. These confused sentences are attempts to describe the dual effect of the plot-character interaction achieved in successful fiction. Perhaps it would simplify to schematize what happens. Appropriately enough, this can be done by extending Frost's metaphor into a diagram, charting the pathways as if they were veins in one of the fallen leaves on the path "less traveled by."

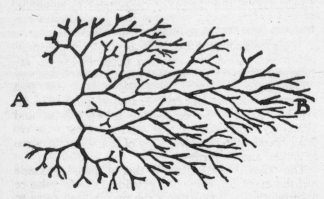

Start at the left, at Point A, and trace the path to Point B. To get there you have to make at least twelve choices at forks in the road. The path you followed represents your life history. To get to Point B, where you are now, say, it seems to you that you've arrived there either by great determination in turning down other possible paths, or entirely by chance, depending on your attitude about such things. At any rate you are aware that each choice you made limited the possible or potential other ways you could have gone. But now trace your path from Point B from right to left to Point A. There are no choices. Looking back, you see the path taken was inevitable.

A story should be like that. When you begin a story and while you're reading it, it should seem as if you're moving from left to right: alternatives to the character's fate and to the plot's action seem open, possible, available. But when you've finished the story and look back, the action should seem inevitable, as if you'd moved from right to left.

Enhancing the Interaction of Character and Plot

It develops, then, that a successful story (and this is as much or more true of a play or a novel) will have two effects which would seem to preclude one another, or at least to work against one another.

One desired effect is that the events and final outcome of the action seem, finally, to have been inevitable, so as to be convincing to the reader, and ultimately satisfactory to him—and so as to evoke related effects such as universality of theme, significance of action, and so forth.

The other desired effect is that the final outcome and the events of the action provide some surprise or uncertainty, so as to engross the reader—and so as to evoke related effects as of suspense, tension, conflict, and so forth. And it is necessary *really* to reconcile these two effects, so that they become as one effect, contributing to the necessary unity of the story.

Successfully combining these apparently contradictory effects constitutes one of the demonstrable excellences of successful fiction. What is used to do it is a variety of methods and devices that can be generally described, but are used specifically according to specific needs of a particular story.

It should go without saying that to be successful a story must have a substantial agreement between character and action. This is a matter of conception. Here we are discussing methods that lie outside the strict character-plot interaction, but support it in a variety of subtle ways. These are matters of technique.

Techniques of Foreshadowing

Foreshadowing devices have the effect of enhancing the inevitability of the action, usually without destroying suspense or tension—in fact, correctly used, foreshadowing can enhance those effects too. What foreshadowing does is prepare in advance for events that will follow later in the story, often in ways that will not be fully understood by the reader until the story is completed, if then. For while devices of foreshadowing may sometimes be very apparent, at other times it is necessary to go back into a story to see what methods were used to make its final effects convincing.

in description. A passage describing the place where action in a story is about to take place establishes the *setting*, but the description can also be colored so as to evoke a *mood* appropriate to the action which follows. The mood is evoked by use of words—adjectives or nouns or adverbs which are dolorous or cheerful or whatever; by use of metaphors and similes; by use of images and symbols—whether snakes slithering underfoot or autumn leaves falling overhead, or some such image less conspicuous and obvious. The very *sound* of the language, as in "snakes slithering," may contribute. Also, passages describing a character's appearance of course help establish characterization in a story, but the description can be colored in such a way as also to evoke an intimation of the action that is to follow. Whether "put in" consciously or unconsciously by the writer, whether "noted" consciously or unconsciously by the reader, the language and metaphor and imagery of a successful passage of description in a story will have an effect beyond that of simple exposition, an effect that is usually preparation for what will follow later.

in symbol. The use of imagery in descriptive passages is only one of innumerable ways that symbol can be used to prepare the reader for the events of the action. Many stories have many levels and kinds of symbolism that contribute not only to the whole meaning and unity of the work, but also to making the action convincing. A broken bowl, for instance, may prepare for the subsequent crackup of a character. Symbols of violence may prepare for violence. Symbols of redemption may prepare for redemption. And there is too the common practice of patterning the whole structure of a story of modern life on some ancient myth or legend—the central symbol of the story could be, say, the imprisoned princess, or the myth of Daphne and Apollo—and the narrative of the myth intimates to the reader what course the narrative of the story will take.

in parallelism. Here the plot may be said to be helping itself. By establishing a parallel to the circumstances of the plot, either by similar subplot or some other device of plot pattern or simply by referring to similar cases or instances, the author may contribute not only to symmetry in his work, but also to a sense of universality in the application of his theme, thereby helping to make the events of the action convincing to the reader.

in chronological inversion. By use of one or another of the devices of plot pattern—by some flashback technique or by framing the story in more recent action, or whatever—the writer may have made his ending apparent to begin with, so that the story is a working out of the *why* and the *how* of the action that resulted in an outcome already known. But this is indeed foreshadowing with a vengeance.

in dialogue. The use of dialogue to accomplish exposition is usually disastrous; but it is effectively used to establish characterization, and at the same time it can carry some suggestion or intimation of action to follow. However random the conversation may seem, what characters talk about amongst themselves in successful fiction is never irrelevant to the rest of the story. When they talk about events of the action it is easy to see ways in which dialogue may help prepare for what follows: the connection may be so direct as a simple statement by a character as to his intentions, or so contrived as an inadvertent slip of speech. But equally useful and certainly more subtle is foreshadowing achieved by an apparently random and irrelevant conversation among characters. Such a conversation—all that reminiscing at the dinner party about the beauty of a dead tenor's voice, for instance, in James Joyce's "The Dead," or the discussion about Lazarus between Porfiri and Raskolnikov in Dostoevski's *Crime and Punishment*—will invariably have some thematic or symbolic or parallel relationship, in successful fiction, to events that are to follow.

in "sequentiality" or "progression." A story may set up in the very first line an emotional effect suggestive of the ending and appropriate to it, but it may be that a sequence of change may better prepare the reader for what is to happen. A series of episodes or scenes is presented as parallel or alike in some way that marks them as establishing a sequence, but differing from one another progressively in some significant direction. One can trace in even so very short a story as Irwin Shaw's "All the Girls in Their Summer Dresses" the stages of a steady progression downward from the elated opening as the couple walks on sunny Fifth Avenue to the depression they feel in the bar at the end. Once established as pointing in a given direction, a sequence of change can be expected to continue in that direction; and this expectation can contribute importantly to a sense of inevitability about the course of the action.

in tone. The author's tone is often the single most important way a reader has of knowing what to expect of a story. In stories presented in the omniscient-author manner, the reader may very often be given a direct statement from the author about what events are to follow. But even in stories where the point-of-view method used "forbids" the author to obtrude his views directly, his tone can be discerned in phrasings, in language, in parallels or ironies of plot, in the authorial attitude implicit in the way characterization is rendered, and in fact in every aspect of the story, from the smallest point of style to the whole ethical overtone apparent in the work. The tone of the story gives us a good idea of what direction the action will take, just as we recognize whether what a person is about to say to us is serious or not by the tone of voice he uses. Tone in fiction is describable: we say the tone of a story is tragic, or it is satiric, or it is sentimental, or whatever. Authors, especially nowadays, will shift tone in a story for special reasons and to achieve special effects. But by and large a consistency of tone, or at any rate a *control* of tone, is the author's best way of preparing a reader for an appropriate turn of events in his story.

in theme. Theme, or meaning, in fiction is of course closely related to tone. Explicitness of theme seldom occurs in a successful story: a story will be much more than any "moral" that can be abstracted from it. Nevertheless, statement of the theme of a story may sometimes appear in it: sometimes in the very first sentence; sometimes in so explicit a form as an adage or axiom or aphorism; sometimes less explicitly but still clearly in the form of a metaphor or symbol or fable. In such a case all that follows in the story may, for the alert reader, be just a working out of what the author or narrator said he'd show him in the first place.

in various choric devices. The chorus is a device of the drama, of the Greek drama originally, where a group not participating in the action offered comment on it and explanation of it in sung verse. Dramatists since have found various ways of integrating the choric functions into the play itself. The soliloquy, for instance, is one device found (although scarcely less awkward) to take over the choric function of explaining a character's secret motivations. Of course the fiction writer can explain motivation in direct exposition (depending on his point-of-view method), and the fiction writer has far fewer problems about exposition of the past than the dramatist. But the chorus in drama also looked into the future and gave the audience intimations of what to expect. Shakespeare assigns this function to a semichorus, like the witches who predict what will happen in *Macbeth*, or to a reliable single voice—like Enobarbus in *Antony and Cleopatra* or Kent in *Lear*—whose judgments on the action and whose predictions of the consequences are presented as reliable. An actual chorus is sometimes used in fiction—there's the group of semicomic rustics in Thomas Hardy's *Woodlanders*, whose comments and predictions about the principals are again reliable—but it is, needless to say, a very awkward device.

"intromissions of the supernatural." This is a phrase of William Archer's. He speaks in his *Playmaking* of "oracles, portents, prophecies, horoscopes, and suchlike intromissions of the supernatural." These methods are again familiar to us from tragic drama—both Classical and Elizabethan—where "Fate" and "The Will of the Gods" are made manifest in many such ways; but they appear in fiction too. Again one thinks first of Hardy's work, for he was consciously trying in his novels to convert all the elements of tragic drama to prose fiction and also used the oracular pronouncement as best he could—for instance, Henchard in *The Mayor of Casterbridge* goes to an old crone and gets "oracular advice," typically phrased so as to seem to say one thing, but actually saying another. In modern short stories we sometimes see the suburban housewife get her fortune read in a tea room, or an advertising executive break open a fortune cookie at lunch. Perhaps there are more subtle ways of doing it, but oracular predictions of this sort, when it is suggested

TECHNIQUES OF FORESHADOWING

that they are reliable, will usually be an over obvious way of achieving foreshadowing.

in aftershadowing. "Aftershadowing" is an impossible word, but what's meant by it is the way in which an author at the end of his story will pick up again, by suggestion, deftly, the image or other device by which the foreshadowing was achieved. What was in the back of the reader's mind he brings perhaps one quarter-inch forward. Aftershadowing completes or recalls an intimation that was presented earlier, brings home effects that were earlier set up. Say, for instance, there *had* been "snakes slithering" on the path at the beginning, foreshadowing; now at the end, there may be the hiss of the steam train as it curves around into the station, aftershadowing.

At the end of the story there will of course be other reasons for pulling the threads of the plot finally all together, for restatement of the theme, for reintroduction of a central symbol, for a carefully written passage of description—reasons of unity and coherence and harmony and so forth. But an additional effect of this may also be to remind the reader of what was foreshadowed for him.

Foreshadowing and Suspense

Suspense as a reader reaction is considered, somewhat contradictorily, to be at once both an intense and a superficial sort of effect. Detected reading a mystery or an adventure yarn, we say it is "just a suspense novel," and we mock any absorption we may have had in it. Suspense is not even a final response to a piece of writing: a reader left with the final response of suspense has every right to throw the book across the room. Most suspense books as such, chances are, are badly written but have lots of "exciting" sequences that follow one after another and lead one into another, cliffhanger fashion, like the old movie-serial episodes. Before one knows it, he's nearly through with the book and then must continue so as "to find out what happens at the end." These are the sort of books of which publishers say "Once you pick it up, you can't put it down," and one of the major reasons you don't want to put it down is that you don't want ever to have to pick it up again. You want to get to the end of a book like that and get rid of it, once and for all. It's a big waste of time: like watching television for four hours. It seems a good, self-indulgent idea when you start it, something you feel you "deserve" and are going to enjoy; but there is scant pleasure in the moment and in retrospect none at all. Also, it strains the eyes and gives you headaches.

But suspense, when it is considered as an aspect of fiction technique rather than as the whole of the desired effect on the reader, can function in literature as subtly and effectively as it does in music. "Suspension," according to the rules of classical harmony, works in very much the same ways. A tone appears as a natural element in one concord and is thus said to be *prepared*. Then the same note appears as a foreign element in the succeeding concord, during which time—while it's just hanging there, unsettled—it is said to be *suspended*. And then when the tone is altered to appear as a natural element in that concord, it is *resolved*. Preparation, suspension, and resolution are techniques which can be demonstrated to exist in literature, just as they can be demonstrated in music. Suspension—or *suspense*, to use the less pretentious term—is not just a cheap way of hooking the reader, but is rather one of the methods by which "aesthetic pleasure" is created in fiction. The reader's "involvement" in anticipating the fictional resolution is no more at odds with his aesthetic pleasure than is the music lover's as he awaits the harmonious resolution he has been "prepared" for.

If we consider that all the techniques of foreshadowing are analogous to the method of "preparation" in music, we see immediately the multiplicity of methods available to create suspense in fiction. Plot pattern or "progression" we mentioned as one, for instance: the introduction of a pattern of action suggests, suspends, and then requires completion. Parallelism of any sort—whether of "scenes" or characters or whatever—suggests, suspends, and then requires a complementary balance. The author's tone sounding a certain note suggests, suspends, and then demands that the note will be sounded again later. The introduction of any foreshadowing technique—whether image or symbol, object or description, language or theme—suggests, suspends, and then demands some ultimate utilization. A "discord" or enigma of characterization may be suspended, then accounted for. Intimation implies explanation: the writer suspends it, then provides it. The reader is kept meanwhile in a stage of what I'd call "prepared awaiting" if there weren't already the swell word for it—suspense.

It might seem that the techniques of foreshadowing are at odds with the techniques of suspense: it would seem that one creates an effect of inevitability of action, while the other creates an effect of uncertainty of outcome. Yet this is just how the "inevitability of retrospect" is achieved in fiction: how it will seem there are so many decisive turning points getting from A to B, yet looking back from B to A it will seem that there was no other way to go.

For it is implicit in the art of fiction that all of these methods will work for the author and the reader in ways that need never reveal the specific nature of the resolution that is to come. One doesn't discern the whole pattern of action of a story until it is completely wrought. Parallelism can be used for contrast as well as analogy: parallelism tells us nothing final about the final outcome of a story until we know what the outcome finally is. What is a symbol until what it represents is made manifest? What is theme until it is rendered? Virtually none of the ways of intimating action necessarily disclose outcome, unless it is the author's wish that they do so. Even the early introduction of a tone or mood reveals nothing of the "why" or "how" of the action to follow.

The techniques of foreshadowing, therefore, far from undercutting the techniques of suspense, are actually seen to be the foremost way in which the effects of suspense are created.

Techniques of Suspense

It seems to me that there are three basic techniques of suspense, often used in combination, of course. First, there is *mystery*, which evokes *curiosity* as its effect on the reader. Second, there is *conflict*, which evokes *uncertainty* as to outcome. Third, and most effective, is *tension*, which evokes *anticipation*. The first is resolved by some sort of *explanation;* the second is resolved by some sort of *decision;* the third is resolved by some sort of *fulfillment*.

Mystery and Curiosity

Deliberately puzzling or confusing a reader may keep him reading for a while, but at too great an expense. Even just an "aura" of mystery in a story is usually just a lot of baloney. Who *are* these people? What are they up to? Provoking such questions from a reader can be a writer's way of deferring exposition until he feels the reader is ready for the explanation of it all. But more likely it's just fogging things up. A lot of beginning writers' fiction is like a lot of beginners' poetry: deliberately unintelligible so as to make the shallow seem deep.

Stories where mystery is deliberately the method, and curiosity about the ending is the whole desired effect, are usually trick stories with wow endings. To make the puzzle or mystery really puzzling and mysterious and keep quickening the reader's curiosity, the author must keep closing the door on all the sensible or ingenious solutions to the mystery that may occur to the reader. Finally the author is left without any answer or explanation at all or with a solution that may strike the reader as (1) preposterous, (2) a disappointing letdown, or (3) a real gyp—sometimes perhaps all three. The more successful a story based on mystery is in the middle, the most likely it is to fail in the end. The interest, ultimately, is not in the characters and the actions they take, but in the mystery and how it will be explained. The trouble with mystery as a structure is that the writer enters into competition with the reader instead of partnership.

Conflict and Uncertainty

Conflict is thought by many to be a basic element in fiction, and certainly it is true that conflict of some sort is present in most stories. Conflict has other functions, of course—other than creating uncertainty as an aspect of suspense. It often has a close relation to theme, for instance, as when two values are in conflict. Its relation to characterization and motivation is obvious. Considered for the moment, however, purely as a plot device, conflict leaves a good deal to be desired when it is made the main structure of a story.

External conflict—hero versus villain, man versus the sea, spy versus counterspy—if it ever aspires to more than routine melodrama soon becomes perforce *internal* conflict. Internal conflict, conflict within an individual protagonist, virtually always devolves into a matter of *choice*. How will the protagonist choose or decide? Will he stay with his wife in Larchmont or will he run off to Florida with the baby-sitter? Will

Martin say the magic words to Jane, or will he let her go the way he has all the others? Situations of conflict are *not* based on choice—Will the old man get the fish home intact?—such situations, again, will become more and more internalized if the outcome is to have any significance at all. The outcome must be made to depend on the character's will: the decision can't simply be left up to the sharks. The outcome of plot must have some relation to character.

The sort of suspense created by conflict is what Jessamyn West is supposed to have called "willy wonty," the reader's uncertainty as to whether a character "will" or "won't" commit an act, decide a matter, do a deed, choose one instead of another, give up or go on, marry the girl or let her go. "Willy wonty" can be a wonderfully effective way of getting the reader to read on: it is the suspenseful reaction at its simplest. But to be effective the situation of the conflict must be developed so that the forces or weights or values on each side are more or less balanced. If we are to have any interest in whether a character will or won't, then the reasons for him to do it or not to do it, the pressures and pulls on him in both directions, must be fairly equally presented. Both the baby-sitter *and* the wife must have something going. All that is well enough, but the difficulty finally is that the more successfully the conflict is developed, the harder it is to resolve. The more uncertain a reader is made to become as to what the outcome of a story is going to be, the less likely it is that he's going to be convinced by the ending when it finally arrives. This, of course, is because he hasn't been prepared for it. Most of the methods of foreshadowing work against the effect of uncertainty. Uncertainty as an effect is to some extent self-defeating, just as curiosity as an effect is. In both cases the writer and the reader are working against one another, trying to outguess one another.

Tension and Anticipation

"Tension" as a word nowadays has connotations of harried housewives who haven't had their Compoze pills. And "anticipation" suggests children looking foward to Christmas presents. It's a tough, commercial, TV world we live in: a hard day and age for words.

"Anticipation" is used here in the standard dictionary sense of "having a foretaste, or expectation of what is to follow." It is perhaps very close to the "prepared awaiting" that we speak of as being what suspense itself is. We all sometimes experience anticipation when reading a novel or a story, or at least remember having experienced it when reading as a child. As an emotion, it doesn't seem much finer than curiosity or uncertainty, or not on the face of it anyway.

"Tension" in fiction though, is a method, not an effect, and we should try to ignore all the connotations of "nervous anxiety." We will use it in a way that is close to its root—*tensus*, the past participle of the Latin verb *tendere*, meaning "stretch." Tension in fiction has that effect: of something that is being stretched taut until it must snap. It has the quality of force under pressure, as for instance when it is achieved through characterization in a "coiled motive"—tightly wound motivation in a character that we know must spring loose on the action. The most obvious way to create it, is by simply saying something is going to happen, and then putting it off—

> Martin was even-tempered normally, but whenever he did become angry he lost control completely. He knew that the events of that day had accumulated on him, had grown finally to be too much for him, one thing after another had mounted up, until finally there had been one thing

too many. Nevertheless he never forgave himself for the way he acted when his anger finally broke out, and he knew Miranda would never forgive him either.

It all began when he went down to the mailbox as usual one morning . . .

Beginning a story this way *both* foreshadows *and* creates suspense. The reader is prepared for Martin finally to lose his temper and do something awful: that is foreshadowing, of course. But suspense is created too. It is not the suspense of "uncertainty" as to outcome: we know the outcome of any internal conflict Martin may have with his temper, and no external conflict is suggested. We don't in the least wonder *whether* (or not) he will lose his temper (it isn't a question of "will he?" or "won't he?"); we know he will. The sort of suspense created is of "anticipation": we wonder *when* it will happen and *how* it will happen and *why* it will happen. Which incident will be the one that is finally too much for Martin? We read of first one frustration, then another. First, the mail hadn't come yet, then when he went back upstairs he found he'd forgotten to plug in the percolator, then Jane called to cancel their date for that night, then Genevieve wasn't in when he called her, then the bus was stuck in traffic for forty-five minutes, then his insecure department head gave him a bawling-out for being late and for something else that wasn't his fault, then . . .

As the incidents accumulate, we wait, expecting what we have been told is to come, knowing we are to expect it, but not knowing *when* to expect it. Then Martin encounters Miranda at the water cooler and she gives him a very bad time but agrees to meet him that night, then when he goes to her apartment he finds Renaldo there, then . . . When, finally, will it happen? Granted a good situation, a good writer could draw it out more or less forever: the thread of tension drawn ever thinner and thinner down to the breaking point; the anticipation (presumably) growing greater and greater.

Tension in a story consists in something unresolved. Setting up something to be resolved and then prolonging or postponing the resolution of it is one way, a fairly obvious way, of putting tension in a story. As with every other discussion of method, of course, there has to be an amount of competence and care on the writer's part, or the effect won't be caused by the method. There is no actual tension in the above example about Martin: it is intended by way of explanation, rather than demonstration.

It explains a *method* of creating an *effect:* it shows how tension creates suspense. The method in a real story is demonstrable: here, we say, pointing to a page, is something set up, either we are told directly that such-and-so is to come or it is suggested to us here, right here, in this more subtle way; but now here, at this other point here, two or ten or twenty pages later, what we've been told is going to come hasn't yet come, hasn't yet happened; and at this point there is stll tension, throughout these two or ten or twenty pages *there has been* tension; tension exists in the story as a technique.

Tension is the most useful and flexible of the methods of achieving suspense. Unlike conflict and mystery as methods, tension doesn't put the writer and the reader into competition with one another. And far from being self-defeating, tension is self-enhancing. The same devices that create tension also prepare for its resolution. It is through tension that foreshadowing and suspense achieve their most successful interaction.

"Agreement" in Character and Action

Character and action are like the subject and the verb in a sentence. A sentence by definition must have a subject and a verb and express a complete thought. You can talk about the subject separately—nouns and pronouns and noun clauses and so forth—but until you put it together with the verb you haven't got a sentence: you haven't expressed a thought. You can talk about the verb separately—about all its forms and tenses and so forth—but until you have the subject you won't know what form the verb should take, and until you have the thought you won't even know what verb to use.

So it is with a short story: You must have both character (subject) and plot (verb) and know the significance of what happened to the character (the meaning, or thought). You can talk about character alone—about how characterization is achieved in fiction and how personality is expressed in life, and so forth—but until you put the character into action you haven't got a story. You can talk about plot alone—about plot structure and crises and reversals and so forth—but until you have a character to act and be acted on you won't know what form the plot should take, and until you know what happened to the character you won't even know what plot to use.

The analogy between the sentence and the short story could probably be extended to a discussion of plural and singular forms, active and passive constructions, dependent and independent aspects, subordination or emphasis of elements, simple or compound or complex forms, genres that are exclamatory or interrogatory or declarative, and so on. Here I want to stress only the idea of *agreement*. There is agreement between all the parts of a sentence—between the adjectives and the nouns they modify, and between the adverbs and verbs, and in a greater sense there is an agreement or appropriateness of all the parts to the whole, to create the exact emphasis, the specific effect, the precise meaning that the sentence is intended to have. But all these refinements depend on the basic agreement between subject and verb. In a short story, too, agreement between character and action is primary.

To use a fixed action instead of a moving action as the plot of a story would be like using a participle instead of a verb in a sentence. Just as in the latter case you get a sentence fragment which doesn't express a complete thought, so in the former you get a sketch, a story in which nothing happens.

Similarly, the character to whom the action of a story "happens" must be capable of "agreeing" with that action. The complex interaction of character and plot in fiction requires a "subject" able to perform a twofold function: the character must have the capability to cause action, and the capacity to reveal change.

Movement of Character

Does character or personality ever in fact really "change"? There is of course a way of looking at the matter that precludes the idea of change altogether: a person is a person and a character is a character and remains that same person or character no matter how he acts or what he does. Even if his nature changes in the most extreme way, as from demure, retiring Eve White to fun-loving party-girl Eve Black or from nice Dr. Jekyll to bad Mr. Hyde, the identity remains the same, no matter how split it may seem to be. All that has happened is that another "side" of the personality, or "more" of the character, has been exposed—this other aspect of the personality or character having always been there, but not previously observed.

On the other hand, most of us speak regularly about "change" in our acquaintances when we gossip about them, even when these changes are gentle and gradual. We say: "Boy, Martin has sure changed—he only had two drinks tonight and he was so nice to Jane," or "Jane has certainly gotten a lot better—so friendly and outgoing." What changes people this way is usually a more or less routine and dull alteration in their lives: they get married and move from the city to the suburbs and "become" dull; they get a different job that suits them better and "become" more confident and relaxed; they go to a doctor and lose weight and "become" less irritable. Such alterations in their lives achieve a gradual alteration in their personality. But if we go for a while without seeing them, the "change" in their personality will seem conspicuous, even startling. Most of this sort of "action" in life—moving to the suburbs, changing jobs, going to the doctor—is essentially nondramatic, even if it does achieve an alteration in character, and would have to be considerably reshaped to become the material for fiction. But the point here is that we realize that these "changed" people are still the same people: duller and more confident and less irritable as they may be, they are still themselves. All they have done is reveal a new potential of their personality, a new way that they are capable of being. Either we did not see it before, or they did not show it.

There seems to be general agreement that as a result of the action of a story something does "happen" to a character. Admittedly it rather smacks of a formula to keep speaking of "movement of character by action." Perhaps it would be more graceful to speak of the "disclosure" or "unveiling" of "latent qualities" in a character. Or of a "development" or "further manifestation" due to the "revelations" of the plot. What one wants to call it seems to be a question simply of what one wants to call it. The fact is, that in fiction, as in life, the effect of seeing a new aspect of character, hitherto unperceived, is to feel that there has been a change.

The Character Shift, as against Movement of Character

Character shift is the conventional term for an unconvincing alteration in character; it should be distinguished carefully from the movement of character by action that we have been discussing. It is not necessary simply to say that in one case the alteration in character is convincing and in the other case it isn't, for while the two cases seem superficially similar, the actual differences are many.

One way of detecting the difference between the character shift and movement of character is by considering the function the character change performs in the narrative. A character shift usually permits, rather than causes, something to happen. The girl's stern father turns nice after all, so she can marry the hero. The tough gangster turns nice after all and sacrifices himself, so the others can live. Movement of character, on the other hand, takes place *after* the action and as a consequence of it. The function of movement of character is not to allow something to happen, as in the character shift, but to show that something indeed *has* happened in the story. It remains an aspect of characterization, not a device of plotting.

And besides, anyway, movement of character involves nothing like the complete changeabout of the character shift. It is not a flip-flop from all-good to all-bad or vice versa (pun intended). It is rather just the gentle, only-barely-perceptible movement, perhaps in only a certain quality of the personality—in, say, the degree of a young boy's innocence, or in an advertising executive's uprightness of character. The movement is just sufficient to show—or even just to suggest, by a change in tone or mood—that something has "happened," that as a result of the experience of the story a character has made some slight, but significant, adjustment to life.

Movement of character is made convincing not only by not being abrupt and startling, but by being prepared for. We have discussed at length the enhancing effects of foreshadowing, which prepares for the character-plot interaction in ways that are to some extent extraneous to that interaction: in terms of mood, tone, theme, language, setting, various choric devices, and so forth. Especially useful in this area is what we might call "foreshadowing of character," intimations given early in the story of elements in the character that are to appear at the end. And the plot or action or narrative itself must be composed of event or incident that is significant enough or meaningful enough or so focused enough that it makes its effect, the change of character, credible and convincing.

Unconvincing alteration of character has always been the distinguishing mark between the higher and lower forms of literary art. The distinction made between tragedy and the lower dramatic form, melodrama, is that in tragedy plot occurs as a result of character, characters determining their own fate, while in melodrama characterizations will shift according to the demands of plot for startling effects. Similarly, the distinction is made between comedy and the lower form, farce. In comedy, humor derives from character; while in farce it derives from the outlandish situations of the plot, which often requires characterizations to shift outrageously. And in fiction, slick fiction is distinguished from serious or literary fiction in the same way.

Slick Fiction, as against Quality Fiction

"Slick fiction" describes a kind of writing much practiced in America from its earliest days, but most popular when magazines were as popular as television is now. Slick fiction or "magazine" fiction or "formula" fiction was always distinguished from "quality" fiction or "serious" fiction—that is, literary fiction. The distinction to be made between them is that slick fiction—whether of the "romantic" sort or the "hard-boiled" sort—always partakes of the daydream, while quality fiction—as Jung said of Art—always partakes of the night dream.

Slick fiction has always been a very curious business: although it's entirely based in misconceptions, its practitioners have always led in expounding theories and formulas of fiction method. The formulas for this "formula fiction" were sometimes as cut-and-dried as the famous "boy meets girl, boy loses girl, boy gets girl" formula that was used over and over again, with only the slightest variations of locale and characterization, in magazine after magazine, year after year. Or the formulas were sometimes wonderfully nebulous, like the almost equally famous "Twelve Basic Plots" (or however many it was), which would present one of the so-called "basic" plots in a single word like SEARCH, then start listing: "Search for identity," "Search for loved one," "Search for the father," and so on. The categories never seemed to have much connection with *plot*; if they had any relevance at all, surely it was to *theme*. At any rate, the idea was that you'd take the basic formulas, provide some characters of your own, add some special background materials from your own experience or from research, mix well, and concoct thereby stories you could regularly sell to the slicks, making "up to" four hundred dollars a month "or more" in your spare time at home, send now.

In truth, slick fiction seems to have been easy only for those who could do it. The practitioners who sold books saying it was simple may just have been out to make some extra money in *their* spare time, or perhaps the work seemed so repugnant to them that they wanted to mock its methods. But, then, writing slick fiction appears to have required a certain amount of belief in its materials. The money paid for it by the magazines was immense; but like writing television series drama today, it seems to be easier to analyze how it's done than to be able to do it. The only serious writer who ever had much success writing slick fiction was F. Scott Fitzgerald; and without disparaging his great work at all, I think it is possible to see a romantic tone even there that made the slick story easier for him than it would have been for other good writers.

Slick fiction is now not much written, at least in short story form. What the magazine readers wanted from it was entertainment and escape, and television can do that now more mindlessly than magazine fiction ever could. As is well known, you can't beat a skunk in a contest that involves smelling bad. Commercial magazines that once emphasized slick fiction expired; new magazines rarely publish fiction at all; magazines that once published a dozen stories an issue, now publish one. The writers of slick fiction went along, with the audience, to television. For unlike serious fiction, which has always been written whether there was any demand for it or not, the whole point and purpose of slick fiction was that it was written to order for a market, and once the market was gone, the writing ceased. To write slick magazine stories now would be like writing scripts for a TV series that was taken off years ago.

The translation of slick fiction from magazines to television was almost incredibly literal. The format was basically weekly and usually involved series characters. The Crunch and Des fishing boat series of Philip Wylie or the Mr. Moto mystery series of John

Marquand in the old *Saturday Evening Post* were really interchangeable in tone with such television series as *Route 66* or *Hawaiian Eye*. All the lovable family situation comedies, where shrewd rural virtue triumphs over evil urban slickness—Scattergood Baines and all that—appeared again in *The Beverly Hillbillies*. Westerns and "doctor" stories were transferred unchanged, and the prime-time television week closely resembles the fiction week of *The Saturday Evening Post* or *Collier's*. The audience looks forward to their favorite programs each week, just as they looked forward to having their favorite magazine delivered to their old-fashioned front porch. But, just as before, everyone—even a child—realizes that it is all "entertainment and escape," just a way "to relax," and that what's depicted is more or less pure fantasy.

Along with the daydreaming and the cliché in slick fiction virtually always goes the character shift. And all three abet one another. A standard slick story, for instance, used to have to do with the daydream of "showing them." An outcast and lonely young recruit would "prove himself" and save his buddies in peril, often by the very quality (an interest in reading, say, or in doing puzzles or making kites—more or less anything) that made them scorn him in the first place. The obligatory scene at the end where the boys show in some way that they not only accept him now, but look to him for leadership, was always played for the lump in the reader's throat. What it all derives from, of course, is the author's daydream: lonely and outcast, he dreams of "showing them" and proving the worth of his work. But what it all ends in, in the short story, is a character shift. Similar character shifts are involved in many of the stories that have solutions that depend on someone having been in disguise: the poor girl is really an heiress; the personable crook is really an undercover agent. The throwing on or off of the disguise functions in the story the same way as a character shift functions—that is, it's an easy device for confusing things at the beginning, for working surprises in the middle, and for wrapping things up neatly at the end.

Moving Characters, as against Fixed Characters

What we have called "agreement" between character and plot is important because once a characterization has been established it ought not to be simply changed so as to accommodate the action (character shift), but must alter naturally as a result of it (movement of character). More than that, to serve as a dynamic or moving character in the action of a story, a characterization must have not only the capacity to be affected by the action, but also the capability of causing it. This is the back-and-forth, one-causes-the-other-which-in-turn-causes-the-other interaction of character and plot.

Something of the distinction we are making here between moving character and fixed character is suggested by E. M. Forster in *Aspects of the Novel*, where he speaks of "round" characters and "flat" characters. Flat characters, he says, are usually "constructed around a single idea or quality." He tells us that "they remain . . . unalterable for the reason that they are not changed by circumstance." A round character, on the other hand, "is capable of surprising in a convincing way." Forster gets into all sorts of difficulties with these words, as for instance when he talks about "discs" which are both round *and* flat; but the real trouble with the terms is that they don't indicate the function that these two kinds of characters perform in literature. Flat characters are fixed characters, capable of what we call fixed action. Round characters are moving characters, capable of movement both *of* and *by* action.

What sort of character will this be? The answer is, of course: anyone, any kind. Any individual in life could be the model for a moving protagonist in fiction. Anyone is capable of changing; anyone is capable of doing something, or of allowing something to be done to him, that will cause change in his life. It really all depends on how convincingly the character and the narrative are presented by the author and the skill with which he uses the methods of enhancing the interaction of character and plot.

But some sorts of characters seem easier to work this interaction with than others. One can realize this simply by thinking of the central characters in successful stories, novels, and plays. Passionate, active personalities are more liable to act (perhaps foolishly or impulsively) in ways that cause something to happen to them. Weak, vacillating personalities are more liable to fail to act in such a way that something happens to them.

Perhaps this is why there seem to have been so many successful stories about young people and old people. Young people tend to act impulsively, and incident is capable of having a great effect on character that is not as yet fully formed. Exploiting this doubly moving quality of youth has made a virtual cliché out of the "initiation story," in which a youth makes a sort of *rites de passages* from boyhood into young manhood as a result of some action rendered in the story: a disillusionment with a worshiped older figure; a first experience of sex; or some incident involving acceptance or rejection. Old people, too, are often seen in a period of transition: their lives are shaky and precarious and whatever "happens" to them in the course of the story seems to have a finality about it that can be genuinely moving.

In life there is a normal distribution of those who are ascendant or active and those who are submissive and passive. Extremes at either end of the scale are few. But, in fiction, because of the necessity for something to happen to someone as a result of action, there is perhaps a more-than-normal percentage of forceful, energetic activists who evoke event that causes the something that happens. And there seem to be more too of those who are passive and submit to their fate, to drift into situations that cause what happens to them.

We tend to encounter characters in fiction at a time of stress in their lives. Anxiety always accompanies change, and anxiety may cause the passive to act or the vital to submit. The situation they've gotten into is too much for them, or is something they feel they must break out of. The discord of the situation creates suspense, requires resolution, and these effects may be enhanced, but in the creation of these basic situations the plot may be said to be helping itself.

The key thing, though, is that the characterization of a moving figure must be deep enough. If too little is known of the character, if he is presented only superficially or in a one-sided way, then he will appear fixed to the reader. He must be presented as capable of having something happen to him. This requires development and it is of course why so many of the so-called major figures of fiction are moving characters, while the fixed characters function more usefully as minor ones.

The Series Regulars, as against the Guest Stars

You can perhaps see better how it ought to work by looking at television series dramas, which have got it all just exactly backwards.

The regulars in the classic TV series never change. They are the fixed characters. The doctor, sheriffs, private detectives, and police chiefs, who are the central figures of these programs, always remain the same. If they are shown falling in love, you know the girl's got to be done away with; no matter how tight the spot they're in, you know they'll get out. Even a child knows this: the regulars can't marry, can't die, can't really have *anything* happen to them.

But the guest stars always change. They are unconvincingly presented as moving characters. You can analyze the guest star's characterization as it is first presented and be absolutely certain that when the program is over he will be diametrically opposite to the way he comes on. If he comes on polite, he'll be shown as selfish before the hour's up; if he comes on angry, you know that at the end he'll be shown as really loving.

Another trouble is with the source of the action. In a series drama, for the most part, the regulars are expected, especially the principal, to do something to resolve the situation. It's the regular who must resolve the action that leads to the alteration of the visitor. It is up to the regular to bring the guest star to his senses, to reconcile father and daughter, to make happen whatever it is that has to happen. This is all backwards, for the essence of meaningful plotting is that a character will be affected by action he himself takes or doesn't take—otherwise the significance of what happens to him as a result of the action is very much minimized.

The interesting thing is that the same backwards conceptions were the basis of the old magazine-series fiction, the "slick" fiction, that was just as popular a generation ago as the TV series dramas are now. In *The Saturday Evening Post* or in *Collier's*, in the old days, there was a series regular—Tugboat Annie or Scattergood Baines or Mr. Glencannon or whoever—who remained exactly the same from story to story but whose actions effected a change (always, of course, for the better) in the life of a guest character who appeared in the story and then disappeared. Philip Wylie's characters, Crunch and Des, for instance, ran a sport fishing boat in Florida. A rich man (the guest star) would charter the boat, but he'd be having trouble with his daughter who wanted to marry a poor law student (someone *basically* okay like that). Crunch and Des would straighten it all out. The formula was exactly the same.

Now obviously we can't expect the regulars to change: there are all sorts of commercial reasons for this pattern of action in TV dramas. If there's to be movement at all, the movement has got to come from the guest stars. But this is all backwards, because even though we only see the same aspects of the regular characters week after week, we've come to have at least some idea of what their character is—we know them in at least somewhat more depth than we know the guest stars. And it is depth of characterization that is at the heart of creating characters capable of movement.

Types of Character

Fiction writers are always being warned to be on guard against "typing" their characters, for it is individualization that is thought to be at the heart of successful characterization. And so it is. But economy is necessary in creating characterization in a short story, and individualization from a type may be a substantial time-and-space saver over creation of a characterization from the ground up.

The search for the definite types of human personality seems to have begun in prehistory and seems destined never to end. For it is a basic desire in human beings to categorize, to sort things out into their separate kinds so as to know them better. Such categorizing is basic to the study (scientific or otherwise) of everything—kinds of elements, kinds of birds and arrowheads—so, most naturally, kinds of men, and women.

The oldest characterological theory of which there is any record is the Doctrine of the Humours—and from the writer's point of view it may be the most satisfactory theory of human psychology ever devised, for it associates the temperaments of Man with the four cosmic elements: air, earth, fire, and water. Air, for instance, which is warm and moist, was associated with the bodily fluid *blood* and a person with a prevalence of that was considered a "sanguine" type—that is, with a ruddy complexion, cheerful, of hopeful spirits. Water, cold, and moist, was associated with *phlegm* and a prevalence of that made for a "phlegmatic" type—sluggish, apathetic, calm, composed. This is the origin of the term "humour characters"—not comic types, but characters dominated by a single trait.

Virtually all of the subsequent type theories have made use of the humour theory's underlying concept that body chemistry somehow affects personality, and of the commonly recognized connection between temperament and bodily type. There have been all sorts of theories having to do with physiognomy, musculature, bony structure, glandular imbalance, phrenology, and so. A famous typology is Sheldon's "endomorph, mesomorph, and ectomorph"—roughly (*very* roughly!) jolly fatties, jocks, and thin, nervous grinds—which referred to skin cell layers right there in the *embryo* where personality is being formed.

But while we recognize the types referred to, they don't seem to include all the people in the world. Nor does all mankind seem to be composed of "asthenic" (long and frail) types and "pyknic" (short and round) types, as someone named Kretschmer once maintained; nor of "The Mental Type," "The Volitional Type," and "The Vital Type," as a person named Bain maintained; nor of 801 types with different predominate "ruling passions," as a man called Fourier maintained; nor does the world seem even to be divided between those lonely, shy types who withdraw into themselves, the "introverts," and those "extroverts" who are so sociable and outgoing, as Carl Jung maintained.

The history of characterology has been a seesaw: human ingenuity has sorted human personality into countless intricate and plausible systems of types, only to have human skepticism demonstrate that the typing really doesn't check out. Studies show that if you establish a rating system from "most introverted" to "most extroverted" and scale a whole group—like, say, a collegeful of students—you would get a regular bell-

shaped curve with most of the students grouped somewhere in the middle—*not* the bimodal curve (that
is: two groups) that you'd have to get if the theory
that there are two types of people in this world were
correct.

Common sense seems to be on both sides of this
argument. We all know or sense that there *are* "kinds"
of people—people who are more one way than another. Yet we all know or sense, too, that no individual
seems *wholly* "a type," and that there could never be a
final listing of types that would include everybody.
What we have to realize is that the only reason these
various depictions of types seem so plausible, when
first presented, is that they represent extremes of a
kind of behavior that is familiar to us.

Types as Exceptions

Insofar, then, as a person in life or a character in a
story resembles a *pure* type—a thoroughgoing, all-out
extrovert type, for instance—he is not "typical" or
usual or common at all; he is far out on the scale, far
from the average or mode; he is the extreme; he is, in
fact, the *exception*. Types, then, are really more exceptional than they are typical. And this profound-
sounding paradox applies not just to a grading system
like the extroversion-introversion scale, it applies to
any manner or behavior that is usually thought "typical." The nice old movies, for instance, used to be
fond of showing us a typical "boy from Brooklyn." But
this kid wasn't really *like* the vast majority of Brooklyn boys, he was *more so*. He was *all*-Brooklyn:
wise-cracking, gum-chewing, nostalgic for Flatbush
Avenue; he didn't just mispronounce *some* words the
way some people do in Brooklyn *some*times, he *always*
spoke *all* the words in a comical exaggeration of my

mother's Brooklyn accent. Like all his fellow members in the so-called "representative platoon"—that familiar group in World War Two movies, comprising a typical Italian, a typical Negro, a typical sensitive intellectual (the author), a typical farm boy, a typical rich man's son, and so on—like all of them he wasn't typical at all. He was an exaggeration, a phony composite, an extension or an extreme, and ultimately an *exception*.

Let's distinguish what is actually *average* from what is supposedly typical. The average farm boy is far more like the average boy from Brooklyn than the "typical" farm boy is like the "typical" boy from Brooklyn. The difference in their attitudes and accents will be far less great. Your average person on the extroversion-introversion scale will be very like your average farmer, your average Negro, your average intellectual. Average people are rather much alike. "Typical" people are all very different from one another.

Types, then—and this is especially true in writing—are used to distinguish or separate persons or characters, to emphasize *differences*, and not, as is commonly thought, used to lump together with a lot of others. That types are familiar is certainly true—but that is because we have become used to writers and others exaggerating the same manners or attitudes or accents, not because there are so many people in the world who are actually like these extreme cases.

Type Characters, as against Stock Characters

It seems useful here to make a further distinction, this time between two kinds of characters in fiction. One I'll call the *type* character, and the other I'll call the *stock* character. For the most part, I believe, the terms are used interchangeably; but there is a distinction to be made, and the availability of the two words, *stock* and *type*, provides handy labels to make it with.

Let us say that *a stock character* is one that we have grown too familiar with, through having seen him over and over in films and in novels and stories and on TV, always performing the same role or function in the *plot*. His characterization is based on a cliché of *plot*. An example is "the other guy," the Ralph Bellamy role in a Cary Grant-Katharine Hepburn movie, the medium-good guy who loses the heroine in the end and goes off with the second female lead, an equally stock character, the acid-tongued friend of the heroine's. Another stock character is the old sheriff who's lost his nerve in a Western. Everyone can compile his own list of favorite stock characterizations, characters who have become familiar because of the way their personalities must be to fit their function in the plot.

A *type character*, on the other hand, is a character cliché rather than a plot cliché. He is what we have been speaking of: an extension or exaggeration of a commonly-held quality or manner or accent. He is the extreme, the artificially thrown-together paste-up of qualities, attitudes, accents, and so forth that are thought to be "typical" of racial groups, national groups, regional groups, occupational groups, psychological groups, class groups, and so on. That is, the typical Jew, the typical Irishman, the typical hick, the typical cabdriver (wow!), the typical jock, the typical society snob, and so on. They are familiar characters, yes—and far from original. But they do represent something—the way some people in some groups do seem to act sometimes—that is known to us through our own observation, through our own experience in actual life, rather than through our continuous exposure to the cliché situations of film or fiction.

It would seem from this that while type characters might be useful in fiction, the creation of stock characters ought always to be avoided—because they lead the author into using stock situations and stock plots. Yet there's nothing that a fiction writer *can't* do, and, actually, stock characterizations seem to reflect a peculiar line of contemporary thinking.

What I refer to is indicated by a basic change of approach in modern psychology. It was always thought through the ages that personality determined behavior, that, in the words of the Greeks, "Character is fate." What you did and what happened to you came as a result of what you were. All the character-ologies of previous psychologies reflected this, whether they hypothesized the determining effect of bodily chemistry or structures or parental love and toilet training or whatever. But the latest psychological approaches—both in theory and in therapy—tend to emphasize *roles* rather than *types*. The part we play in life becomes the destiny that defines us. Transactional psychology, for instance, with its emphasis on life's "games," suggests that people will repeatedly play "the victim" part, or "be" a Don Juan or a schlemiel.

In other words, now, instead of saying "Character is fate," we seem to feel that "Fate is character."

The Dichotomous Stereotype

Differentiating from a type doesn't mean just playing up some plausible-sounding, apparently contradictory aspect. Take, for instance, a couple of cliché-type figures like the courtly Southern gentleman and the tough Italian gangster. You put in an apparently surprising detail, such as the Southern gentleman carries a pistol, while the Italian gangster has a picture of his mother in his wallet. All that does is lead you into what I call the dichotomous stereotype.

The dichotomous stereotype is the natural result of what's involved in creating types in the first place. The trouble with typing people is double: first, it recognizes supposed qualities in a group and then assigns these qualities to an individual; second, it recognizes qualities in individuals and then assigns these qualities to the group. Down South people seem pretty polite to us, so we say, "That man is from the South, hence he is a courtly, courteous Southern gentleman." Or we meet a few of those courtly courteous Southern gentlemen, so we say, "Southern men are courteous gentlemen." Now we know that isn't true. The brutal, dirty-minded, red-necked sheriff of a small Southern town is a Southerner and he's not a courteous gentleman. So first we double the stereotype: "Southern men are either courtly gentlemen or brutal red-necks." This seems at first to have some validity in terms of a kind of socioeconomic schism in Southern life, but then it doesn't really account for all Southern men. Some at least seem to be in-between. This leads to the dichotomous stereotype. We assign both qualities, both extremes of group behavior, to the same individual. "Southern men are courtly gentlemen by day, but they ride with brutal KKK lynch mobs by night."

The Southern man—whether courtly gentleman, brutal red-neck, or both combined—is a regional stereotype. But the dichotomous stereotype can come out of any kind of typing. The second-generation Italian-American gangster has always been a nationality-group stereotype, the opposite of which is the warmhearted boy who works hard, plays the violin, and loves his mother's spaghetti. Extremes—*opposites*—like this can be found within any grouping. Just put the mother's picture in the gangster's pocket and you think you've achieved some depth of characterization, but all you've got is flip-flop typing.

Does it make any sense? Are all gruff doctors really kindly underneath? Swedes, we know, are all stolid squareheads; we also know they're all free-loving nudists. Negroes are jolly, affectionate folk; but Blacks are sullen and mug you in the park. For every stereotype conception we have about a group, there is a directly opposite aspect that is almost equally familiar to us.

Do hard-boiled whores have hearts of gold? It does seem to stand to reason, somewhat at least, that it would be a kind of warm-hearted, soft-minded girl—

someone who's generous and giving and finds everybody easy to love—that would get into that line of work. And that the tough, hard-boiled front she puts on is just a sort of shell that is necessary to protect her from being taken advantage of. Is there any truth to this worn old cliché of characterization? Or any of the others? There is always something both suspicious-sounding and yet somehow convincing about these dichotomous stereotypes.

It is easy to see why the dichotomous stereotype is so often found in melodrama, farce, and slick fiction. Containing its opposite within itself, so to speak, a dichotomous stereotype characterization comes all set up and ready for a character shift. The young Italian gangster can turn okay and save the day at the last minute because we know that he loves his mother and sister; the courtly Southern gentleman turns out to have a brutal side when he has one mint julep too many halfway through the story. With the reverse clichés about the type implicit in the original characterization, the character submits plausibly and easily—indeed, almost invites—a complete changeabout in role. Flip-flop. They are fixed characters with two sides and can be flipped like a coin to Side Good or Side Bad whenever necessary for purposes of the plotting.

Differentiating from Types

In a great deal of fiction, the main character is an "average" person while the secondary characters are "typical" people—that is, "extravagants," people dominated by a single trait or motive to an extent that in life would seem unusual and excessive. It may be that types are a more useful conception for literature than psychology, for in fiction there are no picky bimodal nodes to contest their validity.

Types in literature anyway may really represent extensions of the authorial self—in that all the characterizations may be projections of "potentials" of the writer's own nature. Sitting there at your desk, you may have them all "in" you somehow: the typical Don Juan, the typical family man, the four types of the Russian character represented by the Karamazov boys, even Mr. Micawber with his flip-flop optimism and despair. Well, maybe you don't. But you do believe that each writer's *own* characters may be possibilities of his own self?

It doesn't matter how we think about "types" in life—whether as qualities thought to inhere in all men, or just one man, or in different sorts of groups, or as personifications of psychological or sociological insights, or *whatever*, no matter "what" they are or where they "came from"—types have always been demonstrably useful in literature. In differentiating a main character from a type, the problem is whittling the extravagant back toward the average, a process of individualization.

The validity of types seems to depend on the distance from which the character is seen. From sufficient distance almost everyone will seem to fall into a type—whether regional or occupational or whatever—perhaps into several types. Everyone knows his own differences, from the cradle on. But it takes a while to learn of the individuality of others. From a distance a trainful of commuters will all seem like "typical suburbanites"; but inside they know what a mixed bag they are. Even an advertising man senses his own uniqueness, however dimly, and sees differences among the others. From a distance, differences fade and similarities appear; from a close view, the similarities fade and the differences appear. The longer and better one knows another person, the more his uniqueness will be evident, the more individual his personality will seem.

It may be that what further acquaintance is to the recognition of individuality of persons in life, depth of characterization is to the creation of individuality and originality of character in fiction. Thus we must be

DIFFERENTIATING FROM TYPES

told more about a character if he is to be differentiated from a type.

In 1936, you know, Gordon Allport and H. S. Odbert published a Psychological Monograph called "Trait-Names: a Psycholexical Study," and in it they listed 17,953 of what they called "Terms Characterizing Personal Behavior and Personality." If you like lists, this is a lovely one. How hard they must have tried to find just forty-seven more terms, to make it come out even at eighteen thousand! Here, for instance, are the first thirty-six words just sort of strung together:

> She was ablaze, aflame, aflush, acquiescent yet active, entirely adulterous, and utterly absorbed by her accommodating, accurate, accomplished, admirable, adorable, adept, not merely acceptable but acclaimed and even Achillean lover, when her abstemious, academic husband made an abrupt, accidental, acentric return. Then, abashed, affrighted, and aflutter, she heard him accusing and affronted, characterize her personal behavior and personality as abysmal, so advanced as to be absurd, and so abrasive to his feelings as to seem acrid or even absinthine; although he admitted in his addlebrained, absent-minded, and abstract manner, that she was probably not acquisitive.

Think of it: seventeen thousand, nine hundred and fifty-three luscious, loaded terms that people use to describe other people! What more could a writer want? With a palette like that, surely you can do a little psycholexical differentiating.

Knowing a Character

Who knows how well a fiction writer should know his characters? How much *need* he know about them? In theory, of course, a character's characterization needs to be no deeper than necessary to fulfill his function perfectly in a perfectly wrought story. Sometimes a character gets uppity, forgets his role. We know, somewhat to our annoyance and regret, that Salinger and Faulkner knew more about their characters than they ever told us, that things have "happened" to these characters beyond whatever happened in the fiction the authors wrote. Does knowledge of unrecounted details of a character's "past" or "future"—events before or after the action of a story—help or hinder an author? It might be useful—perhaps just once, as an experiment, an exercise—for an author to run it all through, just in his mind, of course, everything that could possibly be known about one of his characters, which is, again of course, far more than would ever be needed in a story. If you did this, you could in theory answer any conceivable question about your creation.

It's only in regard to fiction, these days, that we speak of "character," for the word has come to have old-fashioned, moral overtones. In life, we speak of a person's "personality." Testing and rating of personality usually commences with the psychobiological factors of temperament—those elements of personality which a person is thought to be born with rather than acquire. There is, for instance, his symmetry, as against deformity, and God knows deformity can be important in a character whether it's acquired or not—ask Ahab, Quasimodo, or Jake Barnes. The extent of vitality is thought to be temperamental, too—that is, basic. So is intelligence, both the abstract and mechanical kinds. You know how smart your character is, right? Is

58   KNOWING A CHARACTER

he in good health usually? Does he have "Broad Emotions" or "Narrow Emotions"—that is, does he react to a broad range of objects and situations, or just to what most concerns him? And are the emotions "Strong" or "Weak"?—does he react violently or calmly?

Does your character have what the psychologists call "social adaptability"? How the hell would you know? Well, give him this test: Is he (1) cheerful or depressed, (2) talkative or silent, (3) adventurous or cautious, (4) adaptable or rigid, (5) placid or worrying? There's a higher correlation between the way an individual will rate on each of these scales than would occur by chance, so from this cluster of traits the psychologists assume a "general" trait, social adaptability. They now have laboriously-achieved, scientifically-tested *proof* that by and large a person who is cheerful, talkative, adventurous, adaptable, and placid will tend to be socially adaptable, whereas a person who is depressed, silent, cautious, rigid, and worried probably *won't*. You want your character to have this kind of consistency, don't you—or don't you?

How does your character rate in terms of his expressive and attitudinal traits? Is he, for instance, ascendant or submissive? Expansive or reclusive? Persistent or vacillating? Extroverted or introverted? Self-objective or self-deceiving? Self-confident or full of misgiving? Gregarious or solitary? Selfish or unselfish? Socially intelligent or entirely lacking in tact? Radical or conservative? Suggestible or negative? With or without ambition? Cooperative or competitive? Careful or careless? Fair-minded or not? Honest or not? Inhibited or uninhibited?

In mock-Freudian terms, what stage of maturational development had he reached when the wind blew when his eyes were crossed and he got stuck that way? Oral? Anal? Genital? What's his "character structure" or "personality syndrome"? Is he the "compulsive personality," for instance—that is, does he have those three supposedly related traits of stinginess, orderliness, and obstinacy? Or is he the "authoritarian personality"—destructive, cynical, and power-hungry? Does he have unresolved Oedipal feelings? Does he still experience sibling rivalry? Is he dominated by the "pleasure principle" or the "reality principle"? And, for goodness' sake, what about his toilet training?

And which is dominant: his ego, his superego, or his *id*? A lot of internal conflict will devolve from this, you know, or could.

What's this character *look* like anyway? At first glance? Later, when you get to know him? Is he actually like what he looks like—that is, does his nature actually conform to what we usually sense about people of his "type"? Can you describe him? His face—eyes, mouth, jaw, nose, hair—and habitual expression, if there is one? Any speech mannerisms, fingernail biting, loping or strutting walk, gestures, and so on? Height? Weight? Age? His zodiac sign is meaningless, no need to know that. But knowing which sex he is might help, and of course you know all about his love-life, don't you?

Where was he born? Father's occupation? Mother's disposition? As a child, did he have no friends, lots of friends, or just one good friend? How was he educated? You know the total effect of his rural or urban upbringing, don't you? Of his lonely or happy childhood? Okay—then how does he feel about money now, and why?

So, can you describe his life-style *now*? Rich or poor? He married and have a family? Relations with wife and kids if so, or feelings about being alone if not? Where's he live? In what sort of town, in what sort of dwelling? Neighbors? How's he spend his leisure? What's his taste—is it different from or the same as would be expected according to the socioeconomic class and local culture? What are his significant possessions? Any animals or pets? What TV shows does he watch?

Take the character through a typical day. Make sure nothing exceptional happens, for that evokes a story. How does he feel when he gets up? What kind of toothpaste does he use? You know how he feels when he looks in the mirror, I'm sure; but don't describe what he sees in detail, for that's a cliché technique now for sneaking in a description of a point-of-view character. Do you know what your character eats for breakfast? How he gets to work? Do you know whether he likes his work, or hates it? What do his superiors and subordinates think of him? Who's he have lunch with, and how long does it take? What time does he leave work to go home? Does he go *right* home? What's it like when he gets there? Dinner? After dinner? What time does he go to bed? How's he feel about it all? You never said if he had a sense of humor.

Actually, as I said, none of this need go into a story. I was just curious how well you knew your character.

Motivation

If you speak of a character's motives—if you ask, "What are his drives, his dreams and fears, what does he *want?*"—then you're getting awfully close to moving a character over into the action of a story. For motive seems to create a sort of potential for movement in a character, to seem almost that part of character which potentially *is* plot. Motivation seems to have a key role in creating sequential, causal action, and formulas of fiction and drama speak of it as the "mainspring" of the action. Writers are always being urged to "establish motivation," to make each character's motivation as clear as possible, this seeming to be a good way of establishing both characterization and conflict.

But motives can be awfully complicated, can't they?

Psychologists distinguish between two kinds of motivation: social and physiological. Physiological motives are those that depend on physical need—hunger and thirst and like that—and they seem to present interesting problems in the studies of rats. As far as social motives in human beings are concerned, some psychologists maintain that they develop out of physical needs in what they call behavior systems—that is, a child's need for food soon becomes associated with a need for his mother which becomes associated with an "oral drive" which leads to all sorts of "food-related" behavior (such as going out hunting and smoking too much) and to a general dependence on others (homesickness, joining organizations). Other psychologists maintain that social needs establish a functional autonomy and that an activity once under way establishes its own motivation toward completion and becomes an end or goal in itself, even though the drive that originated it no longer exists. It seems a distinction without much difference. In either case the individual's motives are involved in a complicated interaction with cultural forces to produce his behavior.

It's true that the basic way we know the personality of others is by their behavior, but we are often aware of a discrepancy between our own horrid actions and our own nice selves, and we can sometimes extend this realization to make a similar distinction between the behavior and the self of another, particularly when we know him well. If it's true that depth-of-characterization in fiction is analogous to degree-of-acquaintance in life, then it would be similarly true that the deeper the characterization achieved, then the *less* clear we'd be about a character's motivation in a story.

Motives cause behavior in life, of course, just as motivation is said to create action in fiction. But it is seldom possible to demonstrate how a motive caused a certain act, in any one-to-one relationship. Any interesting act is usually the result of "mixed" motives. The same act, in different individuals and under different circumstances, may be the result of entirely different motives. And the same motive, in different individuals and under different circumstances, may result in entirely different acts.

Motives may indeed cause conflict, but to the extent that it is two characters' motives, each clear and distinct, that come into a head-to-head confrontation, this is just external conflict and is of interest, really, only in melodrama and slick fiction. Far more usual in literary fiction is the internal conflict that occurs when motivations are in conflict within the same character.

With some exceptions, all the intriguing characters in literatuve have very unclear motivation.

The Stress Situation

Once a character is introduced into the action of a story, we know that something will "happen" as a consequence of it, that the action of the story will have some effect on him. Events of consequence seldom occur without anxiety. Change is pain, we know. Movement of character in fiction may be a far more subtle and gentler matter than all this indicates, but it also may very well take place in some sort of stress situation.

Psychologists, too, have always been interested in human behavior under stress. Experimental psychology about normal human reactions developed mostly during World War Two in studies of the behavior of troops in combat and the reaction time of fighter pilots and the like. More important, psychology has traditionally been interested in the abnormal—the neurotic and the insane—just as medicine has always been interested in the ill. Anxiety is of course the chief cause of most mental illness, and psychologists have developed a virtual inventory of ways people act in an anxiety state, none of them unknown to the fiction writer.

The emotions of a character in stress can be described by an author to a reader in two ways: as expressed or as suppressed. Strong emotion—whether of fear or anger or whatever—causes bodily changes: quick breathing, butterflies in the stomach, moist palms, pounding heart, and so forth. These have been experienced by everyone, categorized and measured by psychologists and described by authors of fiction. The emotions of a character may be openly expressed by facial expressions, tears, sobs, cries of rage, pounding the table in anger, and so on. But there are often circumstances, in fiction as in life, that thwart the open and direct expression of emotion, that keep the individual from confronting or reacting to the situation directly. Pounding the table in anger is to some extent an example of what happens then—it is an example of what is called "displaced aggression," for it is seldom that the table is the real cause of anger. But there are subtler indications of anxiety when emotions are for one reason or another repressed.

A character in stress and frustrated by a situation with which he can't cope directly may be shown, for instance, as attempting to deceive himself about it, constructing one or another of various defense mechanisms that either deny or disguise the situation. Amnesia is an example of denying a situation totally, and it has already been overused by fiction writers. One is more likely to see a character "rationalizing" his reaction—that is, explaining in a very logical way his reasons, for not having done what was needed, or for having done just the opposite. Another way of disguising the situation to himself is through "projection"—that is, by assigning to others the motives or faults of which he himself is guilty, as an explanation of the necessity for his own behavior. Another is the so-called "reaction-formation"—in which a character may be so fearful of his actual tendencies that he takes an extreme position on the other side. Or, such a fear of self may lead a character into total repression of his feelings—a matter of exerting willpower, but unconsciously and unhealthily. The repressed feelings may, however, reveal themselves in various compulsive movements—twitching or blinking or handling steel-ball feces like Captain Queeg. Or it may lead to some kind of sublimation of his feelings—in which the energy he wants to expend in one direction gets expended in another. This can be a kind of compensation—in which a character substitutes success in one field for failure in another.

All sorts of unconscious motives may thus be shown as present, and in conflict, and there are all sorts of other ways too. The character's dreams have often been used in fiction to show wishes or fears of which he may not be consciously aware. He may be shown making significant slips of the tongue or having other significant accidents or symptomatic illnesses.

There is often, in stress, a sense of restlessness and a generalized irritability. Or, there may be the entirely opposite reaction, if the frustration is prolonged: a period of apathy. Perhaps apathy will be accompanied by fantasying or daydreaming—and daydreams, as authors very well know, will often be associated with real-life problems. Frustration also leads people into compulsively repetitious patterns of action—despair is often the cause of what is called "stereotypy" in behavior, an unwillingness to try a new attempt at solution. Or a character may regress and return to ways of behavior that were successful when he was a child, like being sick all the time, or to a kind of primitivism, like picking a fist fight in a bar. Both of these reactions, however, are so familiar in fiction as to be virtually clichés.

In life we feel we know a person better when we have shared a stressful situation with him; people "reveal" more of themselves under strain. While it is true that the real function of action in fiction is to alter character, it is clear now why it is so often maintained that "action *reveals* character." The revelation comes as a result of the stress that accompanies change.

The Importance and
Unimportance of Plot

To a reader who doesn't understand the nature of the
contemporary short story form, that aspect of fiction
known as *plot* may seem equivalent to the whole of
the story. It's inconceivable to have a story *without*
plot; for, as we've seen, what we'd then have would
be a sketch. But it's equally impossible for a story to
exist without characters, or without language or without setting or without theme or without (probably
even) the paper it's written on. Plot is just one of a
number of aspects of the short story; and if it is the
only aspect a reader looks for, all that means is that
plot is all he gets. The modern literary short story
must seem very dull to him.

"Story" in the old sense of "Tell me a story" *means*
plot. But that the whole should have a name thus interchangeable with the part is, so far as we're concerned, just an accident of terminology, for we speak
of "the story of a novel" or "the story of a play" and
mean nothing more than "the plot of a novel" or "the
play's action." Edgar Allan Poe, as first definer of the
form, tried in his review of Hawthorne's *Twice-Told
Tales* to change the name from "story" to "tale," but
that didn't stick, and it wouldn't really have removed
the confusion anyway. The term *"short* story" is some
help, of course. But this continuing confusion of the
words "story" and "plot" indicates the extent to which
the short story has remained undifferentiated from
the simple "tale" or "story" made up to entertain children or to enthrall the old primeval campfire gang.

This purported "origin" of the story in Man's simplest basic nature is supposed to point a lesson for the
modern writer. No matter how sophisticated and

"arty" he may be, the contemporary writer should never forget, so goes this argument, that the short story originated in some such *storytelling* caveman grunt as "Tiger jump me, me get away." I don't want to rig the argument too much, but it's hard not to make fun of it. That "Tiger jump me, me get away" really isn't a story at all in our sense. It is an expression or communication, not an art object. Even revised so as to tell of "something that happened to somebody" conveying the felt consequences of the action, as "Tiger jump Og, he get away; but him scared, no go forest anymore"; even *then*, even if it were elaborated at great length, replete with details of the adventure in the forest; even if it kept everyone spellbound by the fireside for centuries, were taken down on a tape recorder by some scholar and published in *The Hudson Review*—even *then* it wouldn't be a short story. I don't know what it *would* be—some kind of folk tale, I guess—but it isn't the kind of contemporary literary short story I'm talking about.

I go to this length because people are always telling writers that they must never forget that the short story originated in the simple impetus of one man to communicate something to another man, or to entertain him with some "story" (and hence don't forget the importance of plot, is what they are leading up to)—but this has no connection with what a modern author is up to. Insofar as I'm concerned with the author's "intention" at all, it is his conscious intention to create a literary short story as a work of art, and if he can sell it to *The Hudson Review* or *The New Yorker* and people read it there and appreciate it, so much the better. But his intention, or some caveman's intention are of no real nevermind whatsoever.

The best thing to do about the modern short story's "origins" is just to forget them: they're in Chekhov and Joyce and James and in things like the Imagist movement in poetry and Pound's and Eliot's approaches to criticism. Independent of any "traditions" or "influences" or "origins," the short story became immediately as complex, intricate, and difficult as any other contemporary art form, more so. At any rate, it has no connection with cavemen or "simple utterance."

Plot in a Short Story, as against Plot in a Novel

That disposed of, we are left with plot as one of a number of aspects of fiction technique—neither more nor less important than some other aspects. Theme (the story's "meaning") and tone (the author's "voice" in the story) are important in determining the style (both in descriptive language and in dialogue), are intricately involved with the point of view chosen, and may have the controlling decision on matters of symbol, imagery, setting, mood, atmosphere, and other aspects of the story. These are the matters or methods that, ultimately, determine whether a short story will be successful or not—for they represent the potential meaningfulness of the action. Almost any plot will take on a unique meaning (theme) or coloration (style), simply by partaking of the vision and morality (tone) of a great author. One author could conceivably take a plot of another writer and shape it to his own uses; he could never do this with another author's theme or tone. What "happens" in a story, the *real* meaning of the action, is seldom much concerned with the plot.

In a novel, elements of the meaning or theme of the book may be developed somewhat independently of the plot. The novelist can keep his readers interested in the "story" while he pushes his points in paragraphs of exposition or description or commentary—sections that the reader probably skips anyway so as to "get on with the story" and "find out what happens next." This engrossing of the reader into accepting what the author says, is achieved almost entirely by plot—by a sequence of actions or incidents that lead one into another. The reader thus swept up into what he thinks is "a rousing good yarn" may never have much idea of what the novel is about—if such a novel is really about anything at all. This "narrative sweep"—supposed to be the sugar coating on what the serious writer has to say—is often all that readers get even from a good novel. But at any rate it is of very great importance even to the literary novelist: after all, he's got to get the reader through four hundred pages somehow.

In a short story, there's none of this separateness. The theme of a successful short story is inextricably embedded in all its other aspects. The plot of a modern short story may interest or involve or even fascinate the reader, but may also seem to him in some other cases, especially if he is a careless reader, to be virtually nonexistent. There is just not room for a lot of action for the sake of action, for a lot of episodes to develop "narrative sweep." In fact, it is probably quite true that the more superficially "exciting" a story is—the more full of shooting, window smashing, and fist fights—the less likely it is to have any real consequence or meaning.

Let me summarize the plot of a very successful short story, Ernest Hemingway's "A Clean, Well-Lighted Place." Two waiters chat as they wait to close an outdoor café for the evening, and they finally dislodge an old man who has been sitting quietly drinking at one of the tables. The older of the two waiters goes to a bar before going home and recites to himself a version of The Lord's Prayer in which virtually every other word is *nada:* "Our nada which art in nada . . ." End of story. Or rather, end of *plot;* for there is much more to the *story.* There are elements of characterization, of theme, of symbol, tone, and so forth, that make it a very great story. The young waiter mentions in conversation that the old man once tried to hang himself and was "saved" by his niece; the younger waiter has a wife waiting for him, the older lives alone and has insomnia; a soldier and his girl walk past the café and light glints on the insignia on the soldier's collar. There really *isn't* any more plot, the story only runs some twelve hundred words. Yet what a lot "happens" in this story! I don't speak of the great analogies made in the story between life and light and sex and the confidence of youth on the one hand, contrasted with death and dark and the impotence of age on the other—these intricacies are such that one imagines Hemingway intended even such a purely descriptive detail as the glint of light on the soldier's collar as an attribute of sexual potency. Of course, it is these other aspects of the story in combination that give the story its importance, but there is a lot that happens in the sense of plot alone, in the sense of plot or action that moves character. For in the course of the "events" of the story—and they are really no more than has been recounted—the old waiter "realizes" what he had perhaps before only felt, that fear of death and of the dark are universal among those who have the age and knowledge and disposition to feel. He says at the end (not believing it): ". . . it is only insomnia," and adds: "Many must have it." This realization will give him strength to conduct himself properly—that is, according to the Hemingway stoic code. It is, in a way, a lot to happen in a story. There's enough plot to do what's necessary, and no more.

Plot, or incident, in a short story then, is never there *for its own sake*, for its intrinsic "interest" or "excitement." Any action in a story must be justified by its contribution to the whole—no matter how indirect or oblique it may be. Contrary as it may sound to say, plot's "job" in the modern short story is *not* to interest or intrigue the reader (although it may certainly do so)—its job is simply to move character through (or by) action, to provide the *"something* that happens to somebody." And to this extent, plot *is* of course important in a short story, for it is the action that accomplishes the required movement of character that distinguishes a short story from a sketch. The fact of character-moved-by-action does equal what "happens" in the story, and what happens does equal (when "combined" with theme and tone) what the story is "about," which will be equivalent (when *all* the aspects are "included") to the story's whole meaning. But plot is not by itself, by any means, equivalent to the whole of the story.

Selection in Plot

The first thing to say is the most basic: a writer can't hope to tell the *whole* of what "happened" to his character. It follows then that a crucial matter in constructing the plot is the relevant selection of incidents to recount. Even if the writer were willing to start way back when (or even before) his character was born and go right through to (or even after) his death, he would still have to leave out ninety-nine one-hundredths, or more, of the events in his character's life. And what a dull story it would be anyway! And how little such a comprehensive structure would focus the narrated events on the significance of the story. Everyone has read the sort of story that tries to cover too much ground: by the simple chronicling of too many events in a character's life, the author ends up without bringing any of them to life. Even biography and autobiography are selective; the novel is ever so much more so; and as it is the essence of the short story form to be economical and compact, selectivity and suggestion in each of its aspects is crucial; characterization must be deft, often merely implied; description of setting must be suggestive rather than comprehensive; style must be entirely without embellishment that doesn't directly contribute; and the plot, especially, should begin no farther back in time than is necessary to make the consequences of the movement clear.

Just as the writer has omitted many events that proceeded the beginning or followed the ending of the story that he has to tell of something that happened to someone, so he must in the same way omit many events of little or no importance that occur during the period of action he has chosen. He will usually find that "what happens" is composed of not just one episode, but of a number of them; and even if his story can be told in one sustained episode, he must omit some of what goes on. He won't, for instance (and just to be vulgar about it) want to describe each time his character goes to the bathroom, unless he has some special reason for doing so (to show stress, for instance?).

Anyway, of the events of this period that he mentions at all, some he will want to emphasize and others he will subordinate. The ones he wishes to emphasize he will render in full dramatic detail, complete with dialogue and description of place and movement and so on—this is sometimes called "close view." Other events, necessary to mention so that the story will follow, but not of interest to the writer to render in full dramatic detail, he will merely summarize—this is spoken of as "long view"—that is, from a distance, not in close-up. There is, of course, an intermediary method, a sort of "half-scene" or "middle view" approach, in which the writer will neither render the episode fully nor merely summarize it, but will sketch it in quickly, suggesting some of the details of the action. On the face of it, this compromise method seems not to offer the full advantages of either, but it sometimes offers some of the advantages of both. The middle view need not, of course, be "dead middle," will sometimes be nearer close view and at other times nearer long view. The proper selection of sequences—according to their relevance and potential interest—to be done in close view, long view, or some sort middle view, is fully as important to successful plotting as is the original choice of when to begin and when to end the sequences of the action.

The episodes of the action are always in competition with each other for space/time in the story, and there may sometimes seem to the beginning author to be a conflict between an episode of "interest" and an episode of "relevance." In a novel there may be room

SELECTION IN PLOT

for a sequence that is interesting in and of itself but with no real relevance to the movement of character; in a short story such conflicts may be a sign that the story is perhaps wrongly conceived. In a short story, there's no room for anything that doesn't function perfectly in several ways. The episodes recounted are usually limited to those which, as directly as possible, advance the action which achieves the movement of character—which is not to say that there isn't need for preparation before the event or for an amount of realization after the event. And if the writer wants to bring a sequence that interests him really "to life" in full detail, he must then save his space/time by summarizing as economically as possible those events which do need mentioning, but seem unpromising to him to develop.

Only the author will know what is really important to do at length in his story; only he can tell what's of *real* "relevance" or *real* "interest." The story will make certain demands on him, but it is after all he who is writing the story. All I'm interested in, again, is demonstrating to the beginning writer that his choices are many, that there are perhaps more techniques, devices, and opportunities open to him than he may realize. Let us consider an example:

> Martin spent a restless night and was at Miranda's door early the next morning.

This is obviously a transitional passage, connecting an eposide from the day before with an upcoming episode between Martin and Miranda at her apartment. The writer has chosen to summarize the time Martin spent alone in his apartment, restless and worried, rather than render it in detail. A sequence has been done in long view that would have been done in close view. An author could wisely choose to do it this way; my only point is that he could wisely choose to do it the other way. Imagine for a moment that Martin came in late, and, as we know he left early the next morning, let's assume that he spent not more than four or five hours there in his apartment. And let's assume that restless as he was, he still managed to sleep for three hours. About the remaining hour or two that Martin spent alone and restless in his apartment there is much that could have been written.

Suppose, for instance, that when he comes in he is hungry—it is, after all, past 2 A.M.—and he goes to his icebox (this offers an opportunity to describe the contents, indicative of what a lonely bachelor or newly divorced man, or whatever Martin is, would have in the refrigerator), but finds nothing he wants to eat, slams the door shut angrily (does it bounce back open again infuriatingly? or close efficiently with a hollow, lonely click?). He makes himself a drink (or is he out of whiskey again?), and taking his piece of raisin bread or his whiskey and water with him, he stands contemplating his life, his room (describe room?). He walks around it, inspecting the pictures on the wall, the wallpaper itself, thinks of all the things he's left unattended to lately, draws a warm bath to calm himself (no hot water? too hot? or does he fall asleep in the tub and awaken wrinkled and cold?), checks the time again (are his clocks working or run down?). Does he dial NERVOUS to hear the operator's recorded voice? DIAL-A-PRAYER for the lonely laugh? Does he try to read? What has he been meaning to read lately? And what actually does he read? Does he think only now of what he should have told Miranda that afternoon? Does he rehearse what he will tell her in the morning? Does he find in his mail circulars addressed to OCCUPANT? Magazines? Letters from his parents or from old friends? Does he consider his checkbook, and what shape is *it* in? Does he wonder how and why he landed in this situation when all he wants to do is get some work done, get to Europe, get married, get home to Fort Worth? What's on TV this time of night? Does he worry so about not sleeping that he can't? Does he fall asleep, still dressed, in his chair? Does he dream? What makes him *decide* to go to Miranda's at such an early hour?

One could of course go on and on. These are cliché TV-ish ways of indicating the restlessness of a lonely man late at night, but there remain a myriad of original ways too. If the writer chooses to skip the scene, a summary sentence like "Martin spent a restless night and was at Miranda's early the next morning" is perfectly adequate. No need to "do" the scene at all, if there are other scenes more important to do. But Martin's lonely restless night could have—in another story, perhaps—represented the moment of movement, could have been the central crisis, the climax of the story, when his decision is made or when he succumbs or triumphs, when whatever it is that happens to him in the story, happened. Then, it *would* have been wrong to scamp the scene. There are other ways of doing it. He could tell Miranda, over coffee at her place, just what a night it *was*, what happened to him could be explained by him to her. There are in fiction a million ways to do everything, but the important thing is that they *be* done. What is important in the story should be emphasized (or *so* played down that it is somehow accentuated—there are a million ways) and what is *un*important must be summarized or skipped entirely so as to permit full dramatic rendering of what *is* of consequence. The morning confrontation of Miranda and Martin may well be the important thing—how *she* lives is perhaps what ought to be described in detail, what they said to one another after a night apart may be what needs rendering in full dialogue; perhaps it is *her* room we should see him pace, trying to say what he knows needs to be said. Whichever eposide works best with the story as a whole should be the one chosen. Perhaps both of these sequences are needed, and some *other* sequence should be dropped. But the whole of the story can never be told—even the whole story of what happens to one man alone for one hour in his room cannot be *entirely* told; no matter how many pages are devoted to it, something will have to be left out—and choice must be made of where emphasis is to be placed.

Scenes

Books on How To Write Fiction are full of theories about what they call "plot structure," derived from the formulas of the "slick" magazine fiction that was once so popular. And most of the terms used are handed down from theories about playwriting after having been altered a bit to fit theories about novel writing. As the contemporary short story often resembles lyric poetry more than either the play or the novel, these terms sometimes fit the discussion very awkwardly indeed.

Most of what's said about "scenes" in fiction, for instance, is derived from drama theory. A scene in a play usually designates a sequence of action that is continuous, in a certain place (a set), and in the represented time; when the action moves to another place (a change of scene) or if there is an interruption, an interlude of time, then that scene is ended and another has begun. In fiction there is no need to ring down a curtain to show lapse of time, no need to put stage-hands frantically to work changing the sets; but of course the equivalent must be done, with line space or transitional passage; and the term "scene" is used, usually, similarly to describe any continuous sequence or episode that is rendered in detail.

Scenes seem to me a very bothersome concept in discussing fiction, for they are often thought to have some magical virtue in and of themselves. We have said that any episode of the action that is thought by the author to have interest or relevance ought to be rendered in detail—this does indeed bring the story "alive," does "dramatize" it. But those who take their fiction lessons from the playwright insist that a story is best composed like a play, of a series of scenes, each carefully "set," each with its own beginning and development and end, each with its own "rising" dramatic action and its own climax and resolution, each preparing for the next and leading into it. In a short story, needless to say, scenes are seldom units in themselves (indeed many short stories have only one episode); much less do the episodes have their own separate action. And of course there's no *need* to render every episode in detail. All the various problems about scenes—how to get an extra character offstage so that the two remaining can have a love scene, how to get two enemies together for their confrontation scene, how father and son who haven't seen each other for twenty years can convincingly drop information so that they can have their recognition scene, how to provide a big climax or suspense scene for the second-act curtain—all such problems have to do with awkwardnesses of the play form and don't take into account the greater flexibility of fiction. And at any rate they are "formula" concepts and have no relation to a discussion of the contemporary literary short story form.

Undoubtedly the fiction writer has to begin scenes and develop them and end them, but his problems in this regard are seldom those of the dramatist. Consider:

> Martin spent a restless night and was at Miranda's door early next morning. She seemed reluctant to let him in and listened dubiously as he explained . . .

At this point the fiction writer can launch into direct address or can continue in indirect discourse (by adding a "that" after "explained"), paraphrasing the conversation, with analysis and explanation of his characters' motivations and emotions, until he has reached a point where direct dialogue will seem interesting and useful to him. He can render what he wants, he can summarize what he wants. The poor playwright has no such freedom: he must do the whole scene in dialogue. In fact, he must do most everything in dialogue. Thus, most of the playwright's theories about "plot structure" and "dramatic action" are solutions to problems the fiction writer doesn't even have. The fiction writer can learn what he wants from these theories, of course, but he must remember he has troubles of his own. The ability to construct interesting and effective scenes is to some extent God-given in a fiction writer—depending for the most part on his "ear" for writing good dialogue—and there's very little advice about the structure of scenes that's going to help him.

Plot Structure

As to the overall plot structure of his story, the beginning writer will find that a lot of theorizing about this has been done for him. Structural formulas abound. The ending of a story, for instance, which is simply the ending, if you think of a story as composed of a beginning, a middle, and an ending, is thought of as the resolution, if the story is considered as having initiation, complication, and resolution. It is the solution, if the action of a story is problem and solution; it is the decision, if a story is conflict and decision; the repose, if it is tension and repose; the satisfaction, if it is suspense and satisfaction; the answer, if it is question and answer; the revelation, if it is mystery and revelation. A story can be thought of as moving through complexity to unity, through complication to simplicity; through confusion to order. There seems to be no limit to the formulas for the movement of fiction that can be devised: anyone can make up his own quite easily. If any one of them really means anything, then it would seem they must all mean the same thing—which strikes me as a frightening thought.

If one or another of these formulations is of some help to some particular writer in regard to some particular story, that's fine—it's always fine to have found something useful to say to a fiction writer. But none of them accurately describes the *necessary* structure of the contemporary literary short story because in such a story there is no necessary structure. And that applies to even the most basic idea of all: that a short story should have a beginning, middle, and end.

In discussing almost anything at all, it is logical enough to divide it up into its parts as a first step—this book has done that with the various aspects of the short story as a whole (always, however, stressing the actual unity of the "parts"). And narrative structure has always been divided up into the three thoroughly natural parts: the beginning, the middle, and the end. Initiation, complication, and resolution are the terms that most clearly indicate the roles traditionally ascribed to the three parts. The beginning, or initiation, acquaints the reader with the situation in general: usually it will introduce the characters, describe their background and so on, will describe the place and time of the events, and will suggest the basic lines of the conflict—what all the trouble is going to be about. The middle, or complication, is supposed to describe all this trouble: it is here that the incidents of the action are dramatized into scenes, each scene in theory rising above the one that came before in dramatic intensity until after a number of crises a climax is reached—variously referred to as "turning point" or "dénouement" or "key moment" or whatever—this point marking the end of the middle and the beginning of the end. The end, or resolution, is supposed to make clear all the consequences of the action: perhaps as well it will point out the moral of the story, perhaps it will tell what finally happened to all the characters in the story, now that it is over, and it will knit up any of the loose ends of the plotting.

If it can't be denied that, shortened or adapted this is the pattern of action in a good deal of fiction, for better or for worse, it must be maintained in turn that very little of what's most interesting nowadays in short story writing really conforms to the initiation-complication-resolution formulation. It may be useful to a reader to divide a story up into its beginning and middle and end so as to study it and its author's methods, and it may even be useful to a writer to divide his plot line this way too, so as to sort out the materials of his narrative. But this is all somewhat different from specifying that a short story *must have* a beginning, a middle, and an end.

A short story, in theory, and putting exceptions aside, should probably be as much of a oneness as possible; and probably it is something of a fault in a short story if there is an obvious separation between its beginning, its middle, and its end. Insofar as these traditional divisions mean anything at all in the modern short story, the beginning or "initiation" into the situation can often be marked off (as is actually done in literature courses, with a pencil, at the instructor's request) with as few as five or ten lines; the "ending" may be just as brief, and often is implicit in little more than a descriptive phrase or in a line of dialogue or in a bit of imagery. As we have seen, it is probably good to begin and end a story as near the middle as possible.

Beginning

Let's begin again with the beginning. It is certainly true that every story must have a beginning, in the sense of a first sentence with a capital letter, but the beginning of a modern literary story is not likely to do all the things that the books on writing say a beginning ought to do. "Capture the reader's attention," these books say; and readers are supposed to be immediately intrigued by a line of dialogue: " 'I've got a secret to tell you,' Miranda said to Martin"—that sort of thing. "Make dialogue work for you," these books say; and the writer is supposed to sneak a lot of the exposition—the explanation of what the situation is—into the opening dialogue:

80

"You've been living in this one-room apartment on 75th Street between Columbus and Amsterdam avenues for two years now, Miranda," said Martin. "And this is the first time I've been here. How do you like it here?"

"Oh, I'd like to move over to a better neighborhood on the East Side, where you live," answered Miranda. "But my salary at the law firm where we both work, me as a secretary and you as a rising young lawyer, is so small that I can't afford to move."

"It certainly is lucky for me that I worked up the courage to speak to you at the water cooler at work," said Martin.

"Yes, and we've had many good times together since, but always at lunch," answered Miranda. "And this is the first time we've ever had a date in the evening," she added.

Such dialogue does provide an "initiation" into the situation, but it may seem to the reader more like an ordeal-by-fire. It's an exaggeration, of course. But even artfully done, dialogue thus concocted to carry exposition seldom rings true. "Planted" information almost always somehow breaks the normal rhythms and flow of conversation. Characters always seem to be telling one another what they both already know, just for the reader's benefit. If information is to be imparted from one character to another, there has to be some reason for it, some request or demand on one character's part for an explanation from another—and this situation cannot really exist at the *beginning* of a story. Such a situation certainly can exist toward the end or in the middle of a story, where not only some third character in the story but the reader as well may be interested in how two people from such different backgrounds as Martin and Miranda ever came to meet in the first place, and presumably such information could be conveyed there more convincingly. But by and large, beginning writers cannot be told too often: *Forget* "making dialogue work for you"; keep exposition out of dialogue; it's hard enough to make dialogue work for itself.

As was the cause with *scenes,* much of this bad advice about "handling exposition" in opening dialogue derives from "rules" for playwriting that fail to take into consideration the many alternative techniques available to the fiction writer. Playwrights (or at any rate, the people who theorize about playwriting) always apparently assumed (and perhaps in this particular case they were right) that your average theatergoer couldn't be counted on to read his program notes:

ACT I, Scene 1 — Friday night. Miranda Sleezick's one-room apartment on New York's West Side

and hence it seemed to them necessary to drop into the dialogue the facts that it's Friday night, and that it's New York's West Side, and probably even that it's a one-room apartment. Everything that's done in a play has to be done in dialogue, of course. But playwrights no longer use such corny old bits of exposition business as the gossipy cook explaining all about the family to a new serving maid as they set the table for a dinner party, or the monologue phone conversation in which the heroine explains her problems to her girl friend while purportedly asking her help.

The whole exposition business is outmoded now, even for the theater. Faced with a lot of exposition, a modern playwright is just as likely as not to have one of his characters step forward and tell the audience directly what it needs to know. And playwrights realize that the cost of seats being what it is, audiences nowadays have to stay in them through the first act at least, and that if an audience is a bit puzzled they're more likely to pay close attention to what's going on than if they're given a lot of information in the beginning that they could easily infer as the action develops. A bit of puzzlement, in fact, as to just what's happening and where, can often make a play seem, in the beginning, at least, rather better than it actually is— more "literary" and avant-garde certainly, but also more mysterious and suspenseful.

Deliberately withheld information, as a dramatic

device, is at least as old as *Oedipus Rex,* but it was Ibsen who showed playwrights how to refine it almost to a formula: how to hold back any account of what happened years ago—a recounting of which no matter how artfully handled would have bored his audience in the beginning—until the very last act, creating great suspense, the absence of exposition becoming really an effective part of the plotting, so that the plot turns on the unrevealed information, so that when the explanation comes, it is not a part of the initiation, but actually achieves the resolution. Dramatists since have developed withholding information to a fine art, making a secret not only of what happened in the past but also of what's happening on stage at the present; and in many successful modern plays—such at T. E. Eliot's *The Cocktail Party* and Samuel Beckett's *Waiting for Godot,* for instance—it's never explained to the audience even at the end what the situation is, or was.

Thus the fiction writer need feel no real need to create a beginning for his story, an "initiation" into it. Let him launch right in and tell it, beginning as near the middle as possible. And if he does feel that the reader needs immediately to know certain facts about his characters, his locale, the situation—then let him recount these facts as straighforwardly as possible, without resorting to lame stratagems of "hiding" them in dialogue. The contemporary reader can intuit a remarkable amount: he can pick up the situation just as he reads along; he can learn about the characters and their appearence along the way, incidentally and from time to time; he can imagine what the apartment looks like all on his own, until the author has some real reason to describe it to him, a reason relating to the story as a whole rather than just to the plot. A reader is always more willing to guess than to be bored: if he is puzzled, he is at the same time intrigued. Lack of exposition can create a sort of low-grade tension and suspense. The reader's desire to find out "What is the explanation of all this?" can drive him along nearly as well as the old "What will happen next?"

What the beginning of a short story *should* do, what the beginnings of most successful modern short stories do usually do, is begin to state the *theme* of the story right from the very first line. This can be done by a bit of descriptive writing designed as well to establish the setting or the mood, or even by a line of dialogue, or in fact in *any* way that a short story is normally begun.

If the beginning writer will look again at the short stories he most admires and give them a bit of thought, he'll undoubtedly find that the first sentence or two has implicit in it some statement or metaphor or image of the story's whole meaning.

Irwin Shaw's "The Dry Rock," for instance, which is a story about how impossible it is to make a stand on a point of principle in the urgent, urban life, begins

> "We're late," Helen said, as the cab stopped at a light.

Or, Mark Schorer's beautiful story, "Boy in the Summer Sun," which is about a youthful love affair which has lasted long but is now about to end, begins

> Unalloyed, summer had lingered miraculously into late September without a suggestion that autumn was at hand.

The word "unalloyed," so startling as the first word of a story, introduces a system of imagery from metallurgy that runs throughout the story—undetectable until you study it, but effective nonetheless in the way it relates to the end of a "golden" time of summer and youth and love.

Or, Hemingway's "A Clean, Well-Lighted Place," to refer to that short masterpiece again, which is about age and the fear of death, begins

> It was late and everyone had left the café except an old man who sat in the shadow the leaves of the tree made against the electric light.

Throughout the story there is to be a thread of imagery associating life with light and death with dark, and the old man sitting in the shadow establishes this in the very first sentence.

These three examples are from a single college textbook anthology, and the beginning writer should look on his own for similar examples where the first sentence of the story—and the last line too—may have implicit in it what the story as a whole is about. It is not *always* the case, of course, and this early intimation may not be noticed consciously by the reader the first time he reads a story, or perhaps not ever, for that matter. And the writer himself may not have been aware as he wrote his first sentence of its relevance to the whole of his story. But this is one of the ways in which the reader is prepared, however unconsciously, to accept the inevitability of the action which follows. And it is evidence again of the organic oneness of the short story, that it often will have the whole implicit in even its very opening part.

Middle

"Complication" and "development" are two terms supposed to have reference to the role of the *middle* of a piece of fiction. The first is another formula term inherited from the drama and as used here applies to the plotting, not to the theme. The word has little relevance to the modern short story, for the plot—the episodes of the action—of a short story seldom get that complicated, or certainly shouldn't. Complexity or ambiguity of theme is another matter entirely—and there of course the short story yields to no other form in potential subtlety. And as for "development," what is meant is development, first, of the situation presented by the beginning, and development, second, of tension or suspense or "reader interest" of one sort or another by a rising pattern of action, each successive scene exceeding the one before it in complication or excitement or in tension or suspense or whatever.

This pattern of rising to a climax and then descending was once thought basic to the writing of plays. A German novelist once diagrammed it; "Freytag's Pyramid," so-called, follows:

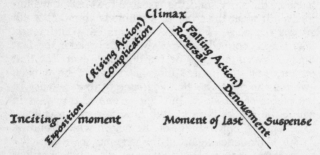

I love diagrams, God knows, but Art seems to abhor them the way Nature's said to abhor vacuums. A pattern of rising action like this can really only apply to such a genre as farce, where each episode is supposed to "top" the one before in outrageous goings-on if the author is going to get any laughs whatsoever, and perhaps it would maintain also for melodrama, where "excitement" or "thrills" for the reader is all the effect the writer can expect to achieve. And the pattern of ascending action is of course traditional in pornography. But for the literary work of art, where the final effect is so much simpler yet so much more subtle, such a pattern of "rising" action is only one of a number of possible patterns.

What the middle of a short story might do, if there *is* a middle, and, I guess, even if a story doesn't have a beginning or ending as such, it more or less has to have a *middle*—what this putative middle *might* do is end with the moment of movement of character. This is analogous to the ideal plot structure of a novel, which supposedly runs through a number of "crises"— a "crisis" being defined as a turn in the action that affects the life of one or more of the major characters in some way—to a final culminating crisis or "climax"—which climax is thought to occur properly at the end of the middle, at the beginning of the end. A short story, chances are, won't have anything like that many crises—most likely, only one, and a subtle one at that. But perhaps this crisis—or "dynamic moment" or "moment of movement" or whatever we call it—should in fact appear "ideally" at the end of the middle and the beginning of the end. It seems as likely a place as any other.

Ending

Similarly, the ending of the modern short story doesn't require a long summary of what happened "afterwards." The novel, though, as usual presents a slightly different case. After having spent so long with the characters, the reader of a novel has become so interested in them, almost fond of them as acquaintance, that he is not adverse to a long "afterward" or "conclusion" that tells how they married, settled down at Milltown Manor and raised children and grew old together. The contemporary novel, of course, doesn't go in for this much, but one feels somehow that it should: after six hundred pages and a long weekend with these people, the reader feels he has a right to know the outcome in full, the details of what happened to them finally. One resents a novel ending with just a suggestion of the outcome.

But the purposes of a short story are different, and the effects to be achieved are different. The short story need only tell us what happened in the story itself, need only make clear the slight movement which has taken place. A lot of modern short stories don't seem to have much of an end at all, really, not in terms of old-fashioned plotting—and this is a great subject of complaint by careless readers. Whatever "resolution" occurs at the end is not so likely these days to be brought about by some final development of the plotting as it is by the introduction of some thematic note: a new image or symbol (of, say, hopefulness or despair), or by a bit of dialogue or description indicative of a new attitude. Perhaps, for instance, the boy in the story lifts his head at the sound of an airplane flying overhead; perhaps the girl turns down a blind date; perhaps a leaf falls, as the first hint of autumn—any manner of such small thing, even if apparently irrelevant, will serve for the careful reader and the scrupulous writer as a suitable and even sufficient ending for a story, so long as its connection with the story is, upon analysis and thought, *clear*.

The contemporary short story writer need make no more "explanations" in his endings than in his beginnings. But the one unforgivable sin in writing is to be deliberately obscure. The freedom of the modern short story writer from the need to be explicit or obvious was hard-won—it was achieved at the cost of alienating all but the few readers capable of understanding and appreciating the form. While it is the obligation of the contemporary writer to exploit this freedom, it is absurd for him to take advantage of it.

Sequence and Causality

Sequential causality is generally considered to be very important in plotting. It is often thought to be the difference between a simple story, which just presents events as arranged in their time sequence, and a true plot, in which one scene prepares for and leads into and *causes* the scene that comes after it.

If, for instance, we see Martin, alone and restless in his apartment, work himself up to a state of wild, desperate, irresponsible frenzy, then we will be anxious to read on and see what the *effect* of this frenzy will be when he confronts Miranda early the next morning. And if he behaves wildly and foolishly in his scene with Miranda, we are better able to accept such behavior, we are more convinced of its reality, because we have previously seen the *cause* of it. There is a back-and-forth action here, of both cause *and* effect, that works very nicely for the writer. Any technique that keeps a reader both convinced *and* interested in reading more is obviously very useful.

But it's probably more useful, actually, in a novel than it is in a short story. Many short stories have only a single scene, and even when there are more, one doesn't seem to get the one-thing-leads-to-another, back-and-forth-forever pattern of narrative of a novel. In a short story, a scene somehow relates more to the rest of the story than it does to just the scene adjacent to it. What I mean is that episodes and incidents will all be interrelated thematically and symbolically, as much as casually. The emphasis is often less on the narrative as such than it is on how the narrative functions with the rest of the story.

Certainly in a piece of short fiction where the narrative is important—one thinks of something as long and circumstantial as Conrad's *Heart of Darkness,* for instance—one incident will perhaps cause a second one and the second one will be rendered so as to make us look ahead to a third. And yet no episode or scene is in there for its own sake—neither just for its own dramatic value, nor to serve as the "cause" of the next sequence. Each incident can be shown to be related to the whole symbolic structure of the story. It is not a simple "and then" relationship, or even an "and so" relationship. Yet each *is* a part of the narrative. It is this double use of scene and episode which distinguishes literature from "literary" writing on the one hand, and from simple "storytelling" or even "good plotting" on the other.

The Frame,
as against the Flashback

The differences between the two techniques known as the "flashback" and the "frame" show more of what I'm trying to say about how plot structure involves more than causal sequentiality. The flashback usually has an explanatory-expositional function; the frame has an integral relation to the whole of the story. They are two entirely different methods, not just the inside and outside of one another.

Everyone knows, from the movies, what a flashback is. The screen ripples over, music ripples up, and we drop back in time for a sequence of action that "explains" why a character is the way he is or gives the "background" of the situation that exists "now" in the movie.

Essentially the same thing is done in a flashback or sequence of flashbacks in a novel. But here the transition into the flashback may be more difficult. I remember a terrible novel with a preposterous structure: it had a man climbing stairs to his waiting wife; every time he took a step there'd be a flashback; the final effect was not suspenseful, as the author had intended, but unintentionally comic. It's become something of a literary convention that the flashback in time be provoked by some sense perception—by the sight of ripply water, by the sound of an organ grinder, by the smell of a Gauloise, by the taste of down-home cookin'—that recalls to the character some perception in the past that was followed by the incident described in the flashback. This convention has produced some extraordinarily beautiful passages as well as many abysmal ones. The finest, of course, is the famous scene in Proust's *Remembrance of Things Past* in which the awakening memory—in this case

90   THE FRAME / FLASHBACK

evoked by the taste of tea and *madeleines* (a kind of cake) which reminds Marcel of his boyhood—is compared to the lovely gradual opening of a paper flower. There the metaphor is relevant to the meaning of the whole huge work, and central to its conception.

Similarly, a frame structure will usually have a relation to the story's whole meaning. The method here is to set a story inside another story that enhances it, or the other way around—or *both* ways is what I really mean, I guess. In the classic or cliché form of the frame, you have a group of characters discussing a matter until one of them says he'll tell a tale that seems to him relevant, the tale follows, then the group discusses it. This sounds dopy, I know; but it's the structure of "Heart of Darkness," and it's how James presents "The Turn of the Screw," except here the story is "front-framed" only, without the concluding discussion. In some frame stories—like Chekhov's "Gooseberries," for instance—the frame is longer than the story it encloses. The enclosed story illuminates the frame story in a case like this: there will always be some interaction between the two parts.

One obvious function of the frame is to permit the author to create a "voice" for his narration (in case he wants to use any special language effects—dialect, for instance), a voice which can easily be that of an involved first-person narrator (on whom the effects of the action will be immediate and clear, and who can be made as naïve or as sophisticated as best serves the author's purposes), a narrator who can be distinctly or faintly separated from the author himself. The advantages and disadvantages of such a method of narration have to do with techniques of point of view.

But the frame construction is often used in other ways and for other reasons than simply to set up a narrator. In such cases the scenes of the frame may be used to provide some effect of contrast (two scenes of a placid, stolid man at home with his family may frame a narrative of his adventures with the OSS in Occupied France), or for some purpose of enhancement or introduction, or because of some thematic connection between the materials of the frame and the events of the narrative they enclose. A frame will usually thus have *some* purpose, will be for *some* effect, will have *some* connection with the story's whole meaning—no matter how oblique the connection may sometimes seem.

Thus it is that a frame must be thought of as a *part* of the story—in a way that a picture frame may not be part of a picture—and hence will have not just a relation to the whole, but be an actual effective functioning segment of that whole. Insofar as any frame structure or the special positioning of flashback sequences contribute to or comprise any sort of thought-out plan or scheme in the arrangement of the narrative, they can be thought of as effective ways in which *pattern* in plotting is achieved.

Pattern in Plot

An author can so arrange the episodes of his narrative as to create a pattern.

We are for the moment considering the narrative structure of the story as a sort of independent aspect upon which certain internal refinements can be wrought; but it will be immediately apparent that such refinements, in a successful story, will have an effective relation to the other aspects and will be of independent demonstrable value only if the pattern directly contributes to the story's whole meaning.

What I mean by pattern in plot is the effect achieved by having the sequences of the action arranged in a way that establishes a certain "order" or "architecture"—of balance, or symmetry, even asymmetry—in the narrative structure. For example, two scenes might be "played against" one another: a graphic description, early in the story, of a man's wife dying of cancer "played against" or "balanced against" another graphic description, later in the story, of the man removing the innards of a deer he has shot in the North Woods, where he has gone in some search for renewal after her death. Two "strong" or "unpleasant" scenes such as these can counterbalance one another, can create a sense of architecture in the story. Again, I am omitting here any reference to the contribution made by such conjunction of scenes to any other aspects of the story: for instance, in this case there might be a connection to *theme*—the cruelty of Nature to Man and the cruelty of Man to Nature—or to *characterization*—any possible motivation of revenge in the man's act, for instance.

Or two balanced scenes could stand one on each side of a central scene of primary importance, somehow "pointing" it for the reader. Or there could be, at stages, a series of similar sequences, each ascending in intensity of some quality (absurdity, for instance, or despair) to reach a climactic scene. Or a character may be seen alone in a scene at the beginning of a story and alone again at the end, in balanced scenes, so contrived for some special effect, admittedly, as well as for the simple symmetry of plot structure.

The frame structure is of course useful in achieving pattern in plot. Whatever flashbacks are used in a plot may be so arranged as to make a pattern. Parallel scenes may be planned to happen to two different characters. Or two like characters may be provided with matched but entirely different scenes for some effect of contrast. Or three similar sequences may be played against one another in some sort of pyramidal structure. Or passages of description or commentary may be introduced periodically according to some pattern—for pattern is not *entirely* a matter of plot.

Nor is it simply a matter of balance or symmetry: an author could pattern his plot, for any wild reason of his own, on the shape of a *tree*, or imitating the layout of a formal garden, or according to the episodes of the Cold War, or following the same sequence of episodes as Homer's *Odyssey*. Any pattern is *possible*, and it's equally possible that a story's plot have no pattern at all. Pattern in plot is probably not a matter for a beginning writer to concern himself with much, but he should certainly know that it exists.

It would seem that the novel, with its complicated plot and many characters, with its subplots and sub-characters, offers a greater opportunity to achieve pattern in structure than the short story does. But the novelist nowadays usually has so heady a sense of freedom from any constraint of form that the craftsman who is the short story writer will as often as not be able to give him lessons in plot patterning.

When pattern does exist in a novel—as it does in many of the great ones, but in by no means all—it is easy to demonstrate. The structure of Tolstoi's *Anna Karenina*, for instance, is diagrammed by teachers with a big X on the blackboard. The novel has two protagonists: the simple Levin and the sophisticated Anna. As Anna "falls" in stages through the novel to her eventual suicide under the wheels of the train, Levin "rises" gradually to his eventual salvation reaping the fields with his peasants. The two "cross" one another in the action of the book. Perhaps the most elaborate instance of pattern in a novel is Joyce's *Ulysses*, where the fact that each chapter is associated with a book of the *Odyssey* is only one of a fantastically intricate set of patterns. The *Odyssey* parallel creates marvelous effects with regard to theme, image, characterization, and all aspects of the book—all related to the whole basic conception of the work—for throughout there is an implicit ironic comparison between space salesman Leopold Bloom's day of wandering around Dublin and the epic years of voyaging by the ancient Greek hero Odysseus. It was once demonstrated to me that even *Tom Jones*, seemingly the most rambling and picaresque and easygoing of novels, was actually architecturally structured—two scenes at the inn are equidistant from the center, and so forth. But this pattern, if it exists, seems too *purely* architectural, seems irrelevant and non-functional, seems to have no relation to the other aspects of the book.

For pattern to be of use and value it must be related harmoniously and effectively to the whole of the story as well as to the other parts. Pattern in fiction is seldom if ever "pure"; almost necessarily it will have an effect on other aspects of the story. Any patterned arrangement of sequences is certain to cause effects of contrast or parallelism not only in plot but also in character; pattern can point ironies in the theme; pattern can mark the stages in any change of mood, or the stages of any change in character; pattern may be involved in any shifts in point of view; and in fact, pattern will have interrelations in effect with all the other parts of a story.

And this is of course why pattern must as well have an effective relation to the whole of the story; pattern "works" in a story only when it is related to the story's basic conception, the conception which determines the nature of all the story's aspects. There is an analogy to the extraordinary refinements of the Parthenon, which were hidden for many centuries. It wasn't until the Parthenon, always regarded as one of the world's most beautiful buildings, was measured and photographed that the "reasons" for its extreme beauty of proportion became apparent: the building wasn't built "squarely" at all; the base was raised in the middle and curved gently down at the four corners; the columns increased in diameter toward the corners (to "outline" or "frame" the composition) and were "tilted" inward (to turn the eye back inward). What had been thought square was actually barely perceptibly graduated so as in perspective to appear square, without the distortion inevitable when viewed from the ground, and so as to accord with the Greek ideal of organic unity in art. This sort of "hidden" refinement achieves a purpose, serves a function, is basic to the conception—and is not just an elaborate superimposed embellishment.

Any pattern in plot that doesn't either "work" with the other aspects or relate directly to the story's whole central conception is merely artificial form, provides only synthetic structure. There is something lifeless, something of the dead hand of artistry-for-the-sake-of-artistry in any pattern or "balance" or "symmetry" or "rhythm" in plot structure that is not related to the rest of the story. Pattern of this sort is like rhyme and meter in a poem that have no relation to the poem as a whole. Pattern, whether artificial or relevant, is seldom noticed by the reader—except that he may have some vague appreciation of a feeling of "order" about the story. But, noticed or unnoticed, it is demonstrable; and if an integral part of the story, it becomes another of the effective harmonies of interrelationships that one points to when demonstrating the story's excellence.

Choice as Technique

All decisions about plot in fiction—decisions about which portion of a character's life is to be represented (where to begin and end the story), decisions about which episodes are to be rendered in close view and which recounted in long view and which presented in some degree of middle view, decisions about whatever pattern is imposed on (or grows out of) the narrative structure, decisions about any episodes that seem to be in conflict—indeed, the whole question of *choice* or *selection* in plotting will be made, first, according to the episode's relevance to movement of character. That is according to a central tenet of this book: that a short story tells of something that happened to someone. But there is another even more basic tenet: that the parts, or aspects, of a story work effectively together harmoniously to comprise the story's whole meaning.

Writing is discovery, yes. But not just discovery of what happens next in a plot, or discovery of surprising manifestations of a created character. It is also discovering how the material of the story all works together, of how a part relates to another part, and of how suddenly both relate to the whole. The ultimate intricacy of even the simplest successful short story could never be imagined from its original conception.

The final whole story will be the result of myriad conscious and unconscious dicisions about method, made by the author. One factor, for instance, that's always present in determining method in plotting is any special aptitude or knowledge that a writer may have: if he's good at dialogue, for instance, he's unlikely to want to spend much time rendering in detail a sequence of a man alone; or if he's had experience of a certain room or city and wants to describe it, he will try to set one of his episodes in it. Any such consideration as this can easily throw any preconceived pattern of plot structure way out of whack, and it is just one of innumerable ways in which one consideration about a story may seem to be in conflict with another. Whenever it seems to a beginning writer that he himself is in conflict with his own preconceived notions about what the story should be, he's probably best advised to go along with himself, write what he "feels" like writing, and forget the preconceived plan. Chances are a new and better plan may occur to him as he proceeds. The decision can perhaps "unblock" the story for him to an extent that may astonish him.

For when a story is "going well" under the author's pen, when it is based on the right conceptual track, everything will seem to be going as if "on rails." The story seems to grow and take form on its own. Everything "works." Scenes which promise most dramatic interest will be seen also to be those scenes which most contribute to characterization, to development of theme, to all the other aspects—and will seem as well to be just the sort of scene the writer is best equipped to do. A scene that once seemed necessary only for the sake of the pattern of the narrative will now seem necessary for many reasons and useful in many ways. Aspects which once seemed in conflict with one another will suddenly interrelate effectively and harmoniously in a way that will seem to the author almost miraculous—as if the story were somehow all on its own working toward its unique whole meaning.

This feeling is of course illogical: it is the author's skill as well as his conception that is creating the story, and many a story has failed to find its successful whole meaning because the author hadn't the craft as well as the vision to see how the aspects of the story could be made to work together harmoniously and effectively instead of to compete and conflict. The "miraculous" way in which a story will seem all suddenly to coalesce will often be due to some adjustment or conception by the author, some perception of another technique that could be used to solve a problem that had troubled him and held the story back. If aspects are in conflict and seem awkward with one another, there will, chances are, prove to be another way, a different approach to the materials. This can be as simple as combining two scenes, or changing point of view, or omitting one character entirely. What may have been thought of as a compromise to reconcile two conflicting aspects may prove suddenly to be not just a solution, but an added value, one that will "lead" the author to additional adjustments and refinements.

There is nothing mystical or miraculous about it at all, although it may seem so. It is "simply" the situation of an author who knows what he wants to do and has the ability to do it. But in order to have this ability to do what he wants, the author must know all the techniques available to him—or he may never have this experience of everything suddenly working. A "natural" storyteller is not likely to be able to solve the problems of the complex item which is the contemporary literary short story. The aspect of fiction technique which is plotting offers a multitude of devices and methods—and a plethora of terms for them—developed by writers and their critics down through the centuries; and although many of them are formula-istic and foolish, no writer can afford to disregard *any* formulation of method that may help him solve the problems presented by his story. If he is to do his own unique and original and characteristic work, a short story writer must have at his command all the methods used by others. He must be able to identify whatever problems are blocking his work's realization, must know all the alternatives available to him to solve them.

CHOICE AS TECHNIQUE

Point-of-View Methods

The choice of the point of view to be used in a story may be pre-made, more or less unconsciously, by the author, as being basic to his whole conception of it. Otherwise, though, choices about point of view will undoubtedly be the most important decisions about technique that he has to make.

Point of view, of course, is in general terms how the story is told, the way in which it is narrated. Defining the term is complicated by the fact that it's sometimes used to apply to the whole of the way in which the story is presented to the reader by the author—the rhetoric *and* the logic of it, so to speak—and sometimes it applies to so small a reference as the name of the character who is the narrator in a particular story.

Clearly there are many different *kinds* of ways that a story can be told, and anthologists and critics are always trying to sort these ways out into their different kinds, often inventing new names for techniques that overlap one another and confuse an already mind-boggling business. The question of point of view can take you right into the basic metaphysics of literature: every story has an author and a reader, and how the story gets from one to another is at the heart of the matter. Point of view may represent the whole aspect of form in fiction, some say; or it may even be the whole basis of the content, as presented; or it may represent the fusion of the two that, according to literary aesthetics, achieves the creation of literary art itself.

Some choose to discuss point of view in terms of "authority," asking how the story is made convincing to the reader. Some emphasize "focus of narration," asking how the elements of the story are unified artistically by the telling. Some systems of categorizing point of view concentrate on the rhetoric, some on the reality. Some systemizers sort out as many as a dozen basic point-of-view methods: Interior Monologue, Dramatic Monologue, Letter Narration, Diary Narration, "Subjective," "Detached," "Memoir," and various sorts of "Anonymous Narration." For others, simply one division into two kind is sufficient: "Internal" and "External"—in which the narrator is either "in" the story as a character, or he isn't—with variations of course.

Commonly, four or five point-of-view methods are listed, the first two being used in most such schemes, the others depending more upon terminology than approach. Basically, then, we usually have:

(1) "Omniscient"—in which the author comes on as knowing everything about everything and everybody. He can tell you the thoughts of any character; he knows the whole past. He may even comment on the story, or he may not. This method is sometimes called "Olympian," sometimes "analytic author." It's the method of Fielding in *Tom Jones* and of Thackeray in *Vanity Fair*. We can't always be sure "Fielding," the authorial voice, *is* Henry Fielding, the author, exactly, but with this method there is usually some sense of "authorial presence" conducting the reader, guiding his reactions to the story.

(2) "The First Person"—in which the author comes on as if he were one of the characters in the story. Maybe he's the main character telling his own story. Maybe he's a minor character telling the main character's story. Maybe he's something in between. This is not as cut-and-dried as it seems: the form used (whether letter, interior monologue, memoir, or whatever) will create real differences, even though the story's told from some first-person basis with an "I" narrator. Distinctions are often made, too, between an "objective" or "reliable" first person narrator on the one hand, and a narrator who is "subjective" or "unreliable" on the other.

(3) "Scenic"—in which the author comes on as almost not being there. He simply describes what hap-

pens. He gives nothing of the past, nor of any background; he is inside the mind of no character at all. He simply records dialogue and movement, depicts setting, makes no comment or intrusion. It's rather like the "absence" of point of view in a play, or action seen through the eye of an movie camera. This method is sometimes called "observer-author"; it remains entirely "exterior" and "objective." You can see it in absolutely pure form in the first hundred lines or so of Hemingway's "The Killers."

(4) "Central Intelligence"—in which the author achieves the story's narration by inhabiting the mind of one of the characters. It's like the "omniscient" in that the author can give past, background, description, and so on. It's like the "scenic" in that the author pretends not to be there. And it's like the "first person" in that we are limited to what one single character can perceive of the action or feel about it. But that character is depicted, not as a first-person "I" but as a third-person "he" or "she." The implication is that "he" or "she" will be the *central* character, and that's usually the case. Otherwise we'd have to have still another term, like "third-person-minor," or even worse, to cover the whole method, "omniscient-limited-to-one-character."

The fact is that trying to sort out all the point-of-view methods into types and kinds is a pretty thankless business. It's fascinating, but ultimately futile. Everyone can think of exceptions to everyone else's system, or variations, or times when an author successfully shifts from one method to another, or whatever. There seem to be almost as many "types" of point of view as there are stories, just as there seemed to be almost as many types of people as there were people. When you consider that just for the four methods described it's possible to ring in an infinitude of changes—of degrees to which the narrator is "concealed" or "anonymous," "reliable" or "subjective," of whether the point-of-view figures be "multiple" or "single" in either first person or third, of whether the whole thing is cast as memoir or lecture or whatever, totally in dialogue or without any dialogue at all, and so on—it seems a hopeless business to try to list all the possibilities.

It seems to me that the proper attitude for the writer is to leave the systematizing to someone else and just rejoice that so many methods are available to him.

Limitations and Advantages in Point of View

Certain conventions, based in logic, accompany choice of point of view. The basic idea is that once an author has indicated by some statement or some construction what point of view is being used in the story, then he is committed to some extent to maintain it. From the apparent limitations of this, certain advantages occur as well.

The limitations are most clearly seen in first-person narration, when the narrator is a character in the story. The "I" can see only what his own eyes can see, he can only know his own thoughts. He can imagine or speculate about the thoughts and motives of other characters, but the author cannot let us know for certain anything that couldn't be known by the first-person narrator.

This is clear enough with a first-person narrator, and even beginning writers grasp the logic and necessity for maintaining point of view in this case. But with a character created by the author in the third person—as "he," "she," "Martin," "Miranda," and so on—it is often more difficult to grasp the strict limitations on perception. Nevertheless, if a story begins with a character named Martin seeing or doing something—getting up, making coffee, going down to the mailbox, or whatever—and if the reader is privy to Martin's thoughts and perceptions from the beginning, then thereafter everything he learns throughout the story must be something learned (or previously known) by Martin, unless the point of view is changed. The reader can know nothing about anyone else in the story unless it is something known by Martin; he can see nothing happen that Martin doesn't see happen; he can hear nothing Martin doesn't hear. The author is entirely bound to Martin's perceptions for what he can tell the reader. These are the "rules" of the fourth method listed, the so-called Central Intelligence, as it is understood today; it has certain advantages which offset these limitations put on it and it has certain disadvantages even beyond the limitations.

The "rules" can be broken, of course, if the violation isn't noticeable, or if enough is achieved by doing so; but to break the rules of point of view unwittingly, with nothing accomplished by it, is to harm the story foolishly—for if the reader is sophisticated, he will see the error and discount the work, and even if he is so innocent of fiction techniques as not to notice it consciously, he will have an uneasy feeling, vague as it might be, that something has gone a bit wrong.

In a short story correct choice and use of point of view is tremendously important as a unifying device, for "how the story is seen" will so focus the *felt* consequences of the action as virtually to become "what the story is." The angle of narration will determine, in most cases, both the nature of the movement of character through action and the identity of that character. By focusing the reporting of action it both determines what it is that *has* happened and also makes clear who it is that it has happened *to*.

Point of view is important in focusing the consequences of action in a novel, too; but in a novel many things may happen to many people, and a "big" novel like *Middlemarch* or *War and Peace* will be "told" or "seen" through a multitude of points of view. Several sequences of the action may be "seen" by one character; then the novelist may shift the telling to another character altogether. Or he may play omniscient author and recount directly to the reader the significance of an event to several of his characters, not using a first-person narrator or a central intelligence point-of-view figure at all. Or he may alternate or jumble or balance these methods howsoever he wants. The novelist may use point of view to focus first here and then there; he does not necessarily use it as the short story writer does, to keep the whole of his story in focus.

Because it is often the voice in which the story is told, point of view also controls a good deal of the style and language used, the nature of the perception in passages of description, and it has a necessary, close relation to the author's tone.

Point of view also has a determining effect on the "closeness" and "distance" with which a story is recounted. Each of the four methods is thought to provide a different degree of closeness and distance—first-person narration supposedly having most closeness, because of its immediacy, intimacy, and authority, and the scenic method having most distance, because it enters the mind of no one, merely reports the action descriptively, at what seems a great remove.

But it is possible to move "in" and "out" wonderfully effectively if you know what you want to do and set up the point of view so as to achieve it. In Faulkner's *The Reivers*, for instance, just to take one example, he tells the story of a young boy as remembered by that boy as an old man. When he wants to move in close on the experience, he puts us into the mind of the boy directly and achieves immediacy, humor, and irony from the boy's misconceptions; when he wants to get some distance and accuracy or make some comment, he moves back into the perceptions of the older man remembering the action. But again, this is just one example of how the limitations of point-of-view method can be manipulated to become advantages. Every successful work provides other examples.

now figure at all. Or, by many alternate or juxta-
instance these methods however the wants. The novelist can shift... point of view... back... here suggested
apply...

When Point of View Is "Wrong"

Beginning writers often choose to tell their story from
the point of view of a character who is not central to
the action—a "bystander," so to speak, "a friend of the
hero," or someone like that, not directly involved. This
is thought to make exposition easier: the reader is
able to learn the facts of the situation along with the
narrator. But the need for exposition is seldom sufficient to make up for the sense of consequencelessness
that often results from uninvolved narration.

Beginning writers also sometimes find it is difficult
to supply background material when they are using
the circumscribed first-person or central-intelligence
methods, so they turn to the omniscient method, ease
of exposition being one of the traditional advantages
assigned to that method, since the author can just
forthrightly step forward and provide whatever information is necessary. But the need for exposition is as a
rule much overemphasized by new writers. If a reader
is at all interested by a situation, he will add little bits
and pieces together, like a stranger at a party, and
he'll soon gather what it's all about.

Similarly, the beginning writer should realize that
in some of those cases where his point-of-view character isn't in a position to know certain details of the
situation, there may often lie an interesting enchance-
ment of the story. For instance, just how much one
character is able to deduce or perceive of another
character's feelings may very well become virtually
the subject of a story. Thus, the limitations put on the
point-of-view character's perceptions by strictly maintaining either first-person or central-intelligence
method can become an aspect of the plot itself. Suspense, irony—all sorts of effects—can be achieved by
keeping a character from knowing some part of the

true situation or by misunderstanding the true motives of other characters. It's often true that the advantages of any of these methods are implicit in their supposed limitations.

When an irritable editor or a kindly writing teacher first points out to the beginning writer the careless way in which he has handled point of view, there is likely to be either a cry of outrage or an immediate capitulation. The young author may be very angry at the idea of his style being cramped by what he calls "a silly rule"; or he may submissively revise his work in slavish obedience to "the way things are done." Both reactions are of course wrong.

First of all, there are no "rules" of writing. Things are "done" the way they are done for reasons, and if the reasons don't exist and if there are better reasons not to, then they aren't done that way. Correct maintenance of point of view, as we've seen, is an aid to the successful focusing and organizing of a story. Choice of point of view may ultimately determine many other decisions regarding character, plot, style, and so forth. It may be the central way of achieving the desired unified effect of the story. The potential to do all this is there. If maintaining point of view in a story seems to be hampering or handcuffing the author in some way, then perhaps he should look again and see if he's using the correct point of view. Changing point of view can often unblock all the other aspects of a story. But if changing point of view entirely is not the solution, then let the author violate the one he's using or shift it in any way he wants. Even the beginning writer may mix up point of view all he wants, but he should know what he's doing, and *why*—and he should realize that he's losing certain other effects that would have been available to him had he decided to keep a tighter focus on his story. If the author gains by violating point of view so as to make a situation clear, or if he shifts point of view from one character to another for whatever reason—if the author gains by it, if there is in fact *a reason*, then the reader gains by it too.

WHEN POINT OF VIEW IS "WRONG"

Conventional methods or "principles" of the craft of fiction are presented here—or, I suppose, for that matter, anywhere—only as possible helps to the author, never as handicaps. They are based, first, on the way things have been done previously by successful writers of fiction; and second (but to a much lesser extent) on theoretical analyses of the ways in which various aspects of a successful work of fiction interact.

The "Question" of Point of View

Two of the very best books about fiction are E. M. Forster's *Aspects of the Novel* and Percy Lubbock's *The Craft of Fiction*, and they differ completely on the subject of point of view. Percy Lubbock states flatly: "The whole intricate question of method, in the craft of fiction, I take to be governed by the question of point of view—the question of the relation in which the narrator stands to the story." E. M. Forster quotes this, says facetiously, "Those who follow him will lay a sure foundation for the aesthetics of fiction," then goes on to say that for him on the contrary, "the whole intricate question of method' resolves itself not into formulae but into the power of the writer to bounce the reader into accepting what he says."

It may at first seem that in this argument Lubbock is making a general point about the rhetoric of fiction—that the relation in which the narrator stands to the story is important—and that Forster is rather unfairly construing this as a specific statement: that narration of a story must be strictly confined to one character's viewpoint. But Forster has got Lubbock right: that *is* pretty much what he's saying in *The Craft of Fiction*. Most of what Lubbock says about method in fiction derives from the methods Henry James used in his novels; and the cornerstone of James's method is the strict maintenance of point of view.

The novels of Henry James have the complex unity and close relation between part and whole that we've seen is usually more characteristic of a short story. In the world of his novels, everything "works" together beautifully, every aspect of his technique is thoroughly appropriate to every other aspect. Lubbock felt, and perhaps James did too, that a good deal of this unity was created by the effective control of point of view. The point of view used determined not only the character of the narrator, but the whole character of the work. James's point-of-view characters are always men or women of intelligence and sensitivity, conscious of fine moral distinctions, with an almost aesthetic feeling for proper behavior—James himself called them his "super-subtle fry."

The characterization of the point-of-view figure thus always determined (or "suited"—for there is a chicken-or-egg "which-came-first?" problem here) the famous and familiar Jamesian style, a distinct and original language, full of "difficult" words and long, intricate, complex sentence constructions, interrupted constantly by parenthetical qualifications and modifications, capable of great nuance. The point-of-view characterization also determined (or suited) the plot, which often turned on a matter of propriety or involved a fine moral distinction. And in many of his novels and stories, effects of suspense and surprise and irony are achieved by the very limitations imposed by maintaining point of view as strictly as he did. His choice of point of view determined (or suited) too the whole milieu or setting of his work—the social or artistic concerns of the well-off and the well-born in Europe and the older cities of America. Point of view, then, had an effective controlling relationship to character, to plot, to setting, to theme—to, in fact, the whole "world" of James's fiction.

Choice of point of view can be shown to have a similar determining relation to the whole of other modern authors' work, but the effect is most obvious and most fully realized in James. It is no wonder that Lubbock—with James in his mind as the master craftsman of the novel—stressed point of view as central to "the whole intricate question of method in fiction."

In refutation of Lubbock's emphasis on point of view, Forster cites various examples—Dickens in *Bleak House* and Tolstoi in *War and Peace* are two—of authors successfully using a mixed-up point of view. He describes how *Bleak House* begins with the omniscient point-of-view method, drops that, "inhabits" a young lady to give us her thoughts, switches and skips from one character to another. "Logically," says Forster, "*Bleak House* is all to pieces, but Dickens bounces us, so that we do not mind the shiftings of the view point."

There is no arguing with success, and Forster is not alone in feeling that novelists before James were more successful than novelists since James have been in writing "big" novels with "big" characters that "bounce" readers into accepting the life within as somehow convincing. Every reader willingly goes off "into" those big Victorian novels, engrossed until the last page is turned. Contemporary fiction provides only slick and sleazy versions of this experience. To "lose" himself in a contemporary novel, the casual reader must turn to one of those "big" best sellers, which nowadays usually means a vulgar novel, steamily exposing sexuality in Washington, Hollywood, or a small New England village. Turning the last page of one of those novels, a reader has the sickening feeling of having done something awful. The reasons for this separation in contemporary fiction between what is "popular" and what is "good" are many, but the idea being advanced here is that there was substantially more "bounce" in the older-fashioned sort of fiction, before all the nonsense about "craft" in fiction came in with Henry James and all those others.

Often in those good old novels there was an omniscient author available as companion, offering to take the gentle reader by the hand and conduct him freely from place to place, from character to character, wherever the action was, explaining what each character was up to, who was good and who was bad and who was in-between and why, neglecting nothing to get the reader interested and involved in what was happening, explaining and interpreting it all, and generally making everything clear.

Even careful readers find that there is a good deal of ambiguity—much of it surely not intentional—in the work of James and of those who follow his point-of-view method. There are famously two entirely different "ways" of reading James's *Turn of the Screw*, for instance: the governess's point of view is maintained so strictly that a case can be made that the specters in the story are not real, but imagined, products of her sexual fantasies. In fact, there is much legitimate confusion as to just how the events of much modern fiction should be understood by the reader—confusion that would vanish instantly if the author were there to step forward and explain the truth of the situation and say a word or two about what we're supposed to think of it.

Henry James himself spoke of English fiction as "a paradise of loose ends," referring not to ambiguity but to all the easiness and pleasure and leisureliness and clarity of the old hit-or-miss methods of narration that have now been swept away—so the argument goes—by enthusiasm for the newer-fangled "tight" kind of fiction, where excellence seems to depend on craft, not content.

The question of point of view is central to this continuing discussion about the effect of craft in fiction. Of shiftings in point of view, Forster says further that "critics are more apt to object than readers" and that "since the problem of a point of view certainly is peculiar to the novel" (drama doesn't have it) the critics have "rather over-stressed it" in an attempt to establish fiction as a separate art form.

And it is true that Lubbock's book is called *The Craft of Fiction* and that the collection R. P. Blackmur made of James's prefaces to his novels is called *The Art of the Novel*. Clearly both James and Lubbock do assume that the effects of fiction (including, presumably, the effect of "bouncing" the reader into believing the story) are achieved by "craft" or "art"—at any rate, by *method*. They *do* assume that fiction is an art form, that it *will* have its own techniques, problems, and methods, and that as point of view *is* in fact unique to fiction it may very well be at the center of "the whole intricate question of method in the craft of fiction."

Point of View and "Involvement"

Perhaps it would be well to state the obvious here: *It is by method that effects are achieved.* Not, perhaps, methodically calculated methods; not even, perhaps, methods which an author may be totally aware of using; but methods that are demonstrable in the work.

How, anyway, *is* a reader "bounced" into accepting what the author says? How is this involvement of the reader achieved? A lot of modern writers don't even want this effect, and a short story will always provide a good deal less of it than will a novel.

But if a writer does want the reader "in," wants him to "enter" the world of his fiction, there are certainly ways of getting him there. One is the system of promises of action to come that we discussed in terms of foreshadowing and suspense. Another will always be the basic character-plot interaction: having characters do things that are on the one hand surprising and interesting, and on the other hand convincing and credible. But the most important aspect of the sensation of involvement, considered just as an effect, is the reader's loss of sense of self. The way a reader "loses himself" in a book is by shutting off his regular world and entering the world of the book. It is more a question of "enclosure" than it is of "bounce."

We must imagine a reader with no distractions; or, if that is unimaginable in this day and age, a reader in a chair with a book or magazine, with nothing much bothering him for the space of time it will take to read what we have in mind for him. He *will*, of course, have some distractions; everyone does. Minor worries: errands unrun, work postponed, things to do, perhaps even the feeling that there's something else he ought to be reading. Never mind, he starts with us.

But how will we begin with him? We know that the first paragraph, the very first sentence, must do special work. He has not yet begun to concentrate and read carefully, and good writing may be wasted here; but it is especially needed here. He will not be concentrated here, perhaps, but he will not be involved yet either. He will be critical; we must be careful. No belief or faith is yet established. You need some confidence in a person before you go on a journey with him. Once he starts with us, he will be in motion and we can keep him in motion more easily.

As he reads on, one by one little pieces of his consciousness of self drop from him, a worry there, a distraction there, a sense that the chair's uncomfortable there; a memory of how he must stop reading in time to phone Miranda about dinner is replaced by a memory of what E.M. Forster elsewhere calls "a half-explained gesture" made by one of our characters. His memory fills gradually with our mysteries, our tensions take the place of his anxieties, our conflicts replace his worries, our point of view replaces his consciousness, our narrator's voice is the only sound he hears, what our narrator shows him is all he sees. He is absorbed, involved, enclosed in the world of the book.

Again: this is not *necessarily* a good thing. Modern fiction especially wants considerably more distance from the reader than this. But we have seen that point of view is the most important way of establishing closeness and distance; and if what one wants is the effect of enclosure, the method of presenting the narrative to the reader has got to be the most determining thing.

Forster says that "bouncing" the reader is more important in fiction than point of view. But even if one agrees about the importance of "bounce," the question is, how to do it? Bounce and point of view are not comparable. The first is an end, the second is a means; the first is an effect, the second is a method.

Thus the *real* question is: what *methods* can the author best use to create illusion, or enclosure, or bounce, or reader involvement, or whatever one calls it? One of the most effective methods of bringing a story alive, and together, and to the point, is to get the point of view right. Correct use of point of view may not be all it takes to bounce a reader into believing a story, but it won't bounce him out either.

Even Forster doesn't say that Dickens in *Bleak House* and Tolstoi in *War and Peace* are successful *because* point of view in these novels is "all to pieces." "Dickens bounces us," he says, "*so that we do not mind* the shiftings of the view point." And in logic it must be true that either the author gained something by violating point of view or shifting it, or the book would have been better if he hadn't. In *David Copperfield* and *Great Expectations* Dickens holds point of view fairly firmly (they are first-person point of view), and they are certainly just as bouncy books as *Bleak House*—infinitely more bouncy, most people feel. In *War and Peace* Tolstoi does shift point of view from chapter to chapter, but in each chapter he is focusing on a different character, or different set of characters. The structure of *War and Peace* is altogether different from that of a Henry James novel—it has many plots, not just one, and many characters, and Tolstoi shifts so as to focus the unifying power of point of view on each in turn. Shifting point of view as the action shifts from one character to another is a necessary practice in novels where many characters are involved, and such shiftings prove the effectiveness and usefulness of point of view, not the opposite.

When Forster scoffs at those who follow Lubbock in attempting to "lay a sure foundation for the aesthetics of fiction," he is undoubtedly correct in mocking what could only be a foolish project. No theory of fiction could embrace all the various sorts of method used in all the successful stories and novels that have been written, much less in all those original works that will be written in years to come. But this is not to say that intensive internal analysis of some of the methods successfully used by writers in the past to bounce or involve or amuse their readers hasn't a great value both to current readers and future writers. The almost mathematical precision with which Percy Lubbock discusses the question of point of view in *The Craft of Fiction* is one of the best examples we have of this sort of analysis in action; and James's prefaces themselves are also very precise and informative about the effects of technique.

But Henry James discusses technique as he used it to solve particular problems in his own novels and stories; and Lubbock's theories about method are based, as we said, primarily on the methods James used. Most of what is said about the effects of method or the usefulness of technique is not as abstract as it sounds. Theories about method derive for the most part from specific examples of their successful use by specific authors in specific novels or stories. The more they are generalized to cover a variety of instances of successful use, the less accurate they are likely to be as to specific effect. The beginning writer must realize that although a successful author, or even a succession of successful authors, may have repeatedly used a given method to solve a given problem, he can't count on it working for himself. Problems always tend to look more alike than solutions. Successful solutions are usually unique—both individual and original.

Once again: no "rule" of writing exists. Not a single one. Nor should suggestions about the general or specific effectiveness of any given method in any hypothetical case ever be construed as advising a beginning author away from a full exploitation of everything that's been done in fiction before, much less from the myriad original methods and manners of writing fiction that will be found in the future. One original method and manner of the fiction of the future may be characteristically his own.

The "Moved" Character and Point of View

The decision about which character will "get" the point of view in a story is usually part of the author's original conception, seldom a matter of conscious choice. Nevertheless, several considerations pertain. One central one is whether the point-of-view character, as created or chosen, is compatible with the author's own "vision" and "voice," enough like him to make for easy narration. Another consideration, this time from the plotting, is whether the character can logically be in all the necessary places at the right time so as to be able to recount what's needed. These are only *considerations*, of course, among many; and there seems to be nothing that actually *controls* the choice.

For instance, considerations from characterization might suggest that an adult, perceptive, fine-conscience consciousness might be the best way to present the story and its implications, and indeed this works splendidly for writers like Henry James and Edith Wharton. But writers like Anderson, Twain, Faulkner, and Hemingway show how perception and narration by a naïve and eloquently inarticulate character—perhaps, for instance, a youth—can far better achieve their story's intention, can in fact become the very point of their story through the irony achieved by some discrepancy of realization.

Thus, where point of view falls in successful fiction seems felicitiously random, a little like where God chooses to bestow miraculous perception in life—whether on a shepherdess or a king, a scholar or a fool.

There is, however, one consideration about where point of view shall fall that seems to me to devolve so inexorably from the dynamics of fiction that even the best authors get into trouble when they fail to take it into account and much fiction by lesser writers fails to succeed just because of neglecting it.

The essential dynamic of fiction, we have said, is that character is moved by action. We have called the character to whom the events of the narrative have consequence the "moved" character. It is my belief that the moved character and the point-of-view character, in successful fiction, will prove to be one and the same.

This may seem to be so inevitable as to be obvious, but I don't believe anyone has pointed it out before. Many writers never realize it or sense its naturalness. Even major authors sometimes recognize only the effects of it and not the theory.

Henry James, for instance, discovered this for himself when he was writing *Roderick Hudson*. James later became the absolute master of technique in fiction; but, as he explains in his preface to the New York edition, thirty-five years later, this was his first attempt at writing a novel, and he couldn't seem to render convincingly the stages of the disintegration of his central figure, the young sculptor Roderick Hudson, as described by his point-of-view character, Rowland Mallet. James mentions various solutions that he considered, then describes "what really saved" the book. "My subject," he says, "had defined itself—and this in spite of the title of the book—as not directly, in the least, my young sculptor's adventure." The "centre of interest," he discovered, was "in Rowland Mallet's consciousness, and the drama is the very drama of that consciousness . . . of what 'happened' to him."

Thus what "happened" in the novel is not the disintegration of Roderick Hudson, but what happened to the point-of-view character, Rowland Mallet, as a result of his perception of this disintegartion. As R. P. Blackmur says, in his introduction to James's *Art of the Novel:* "James never put his readers in direct contact with his subjects; he believed it was impossible to do so, because *his subject really was not what happened but what someone felt about what happened,* and this could be directly known only through an intermediate intelligence."

This, I believe, is what will always be the case in successful fiction: that either the character moved by the action of the story will be the point-of-view character, or else the point-of-view character will *become* the character moved by the action. Call it "Hills' Law."

Another example is what happened to Norman Mailer when he was writing *The Deer Park*. "Originally," he tells us in *Advertisements for Myself*, "*The Deer Park* had been about a movie director and a girl with whom he had a bad affair, and it was told by a sensitive but faceless young man. In changing the young man, I . . . put a disproportion upon [the book] because my narrator became too interesting, and not enough happened to him in the second half of the book, and . . . before I was finished, I saw a way to write another book altogether."

Almost any successful novel or short story will provide proof of this thesis—that the point-of-view character is the moved character or will become so—but let me just refer as examples to two short novels everyone interested in fiction will know: Scott Fitzgerald's *The Great Gatsby* and Joseph Conrad's *Heart of Darkness*.

The central figure in *Gatsby* may be the title character, but the point-of-view figure is of course the narrator, Nick Carraway, and the book eventually focuses on the effects of the action on him. This is made very clear at the beginning, in several key sections in the middle, but most forcefully at the end: Gatsby can lie out there, shot dead on a raft in his pool; Daisy and Tom can cozily eat chicken in the kitchen forever; it's clear they haven't changed. What's "happened" in the novel is what's happened to Nick, the movement by action that makes him decide to return to the Midwest at the end, with all the associations that has for him.

Heart of Darkness also seems at first to be about what happened to someone other than the point-of-view character; supposedly it is about a character named Kurtz and what he experienced in deepest Africa. "I don't want to bother you much with what happened to me personally," begins the narrator, Marlow. But then he goes right on. "Yet to understand the effect of it on me you ought to know how I got out there, what I saw, how I went up that river to the place where I first met the poor chap." And by the time the story is over it is obvious that what's important is what "happened" to the narrator, Marlow, what *he* experienced (from Kurtz's experience), as far upriver into the heart of darkness as it is possible to go, about the way good and evil are mixed in human actions, so that it is possible for him—he who hates a lie, as it is made clear at the beginning—to tell a lie at the end.

In *Lord Jim,* where Marlow also appears as narrator, the point-of-view structure is more complicated, but the same thesis applies. Where the action is of consequence to Jim, Jim himself narrates it in long first-person sequences which Marlow then reports as he heard it to his assembled listeners, one of whom, it is suggested—the unidentified "privileged man"—wrote it all down.

Even in novels where point of view shifts from one character to another, the thesis remains valid within the sections. In an X-shaped novel like *Anna Karenina,* for instance, in those sections where the subject is the decline of Anna, the point of view is likely to be Anna's; where the subject is the rising of Levin, the point of view of those sections is his.

This effect can be noted in reading any novel or short story. To test it in writing, a useful exercise for a beginning writer is to tell a story à la *Rashomon*—that is, tell the same story from the point of view of each participant. Immediately the writer will see how the significance of the action changes to become of consequence to the narrator.

This fact of fiction corresponds naturally to a fact of life. As a character in John Barth's marvelous novel *The End of the Road* says: "Everyone is necessarily the hero of his own life story." Then he gives this example.

Suppose you're an usher in a wedding. From the groom's viewpoint, he's the major character; the others play supporting parts, even the bride. From your viewpoint, though, the wedding is a minor episode in the very interesting history of *your* life, and the bride and groom both are minor figures . . . Every member of the congregation at the wedding sees himself as the major character.

So, the fact is, as Barth's character goes on to say, that "Fiction isn't a lie at all, but a true representation of the distortion that everyone makes of life." And that distortion, that shaping of the materials of the narration by the point-of-view character, is inevitable, because "Not only are we the heroes of our own life stories—we're the ones who conceive the story, and give other people the essences of minor characters."

The Focusing Power of Point of View

Many novels and short stories are undoubtedly written neglecting the relation between angle of narration and focus of narration. The unsuccessful ones often seem to just sit there, the action having even less impact on the reader than on the unmoved point-of-view character. To start a narrator-perceiver out on a long account of how an action affects someone else is virtually to ask for trouble in the writing. If the teller of the story doesn't feel the consequences of the action, how can the reader be expected to? If what "happens" hasn't happened to him, then it's as if it hadn't happened at all.

But then, in good stories by good writers, one often sees a point-of-view method that started off "wrong"— or at least indirectly—being worked around to focus on the real consequences of the action. And it's fascinating to notice this, once one's started to read with this sense of the necessary dynamics of fiction.

Take the beginning of Hemingway's "The Killers," for instance. When the two killers enter the lunch room, the story is presented almost as if it were a play—that is, dialogue plus a few stage directions, like this: "'You better go around, bright boy,' said Al. Nick went around behind the counter." This is the pure "scenic" method. We don't enter the mind of any of the characters, ever in the story. But we follow Nick later, as he goes to warn the ex-prizefighter about the killers and then returns to the restaurant. It is only by being with Nick that we could be told all that we are told. We learn only what he learns. And then at the end we learn his reaction: "I can't stand to think about him waiting in the room and knowing he's going to get it. It's too damn awful." And we see that he has been moved by the action: "'I'm going to get out of this town,' Nick said." We realize that it is Nick's story, that what happened in it is what's happened to him.

You can see the same shift in point of view and consequence in "A Clean, Well-Lighted Place." The story begins semi-scenic, then it becomes the older waiter's story; it is he who is moved by it at the end.

Or take a far more confused case of shifting point of view, D. H. Lawrence's "The Horse Dealer's Daughter," for instance, where point-of-view conventions seem not to be observed at all. The story opens with three brothers and one sister at the breakfast table, on the day they must give up their father's farm. Point of view begins in the older brother's consciousness, and we're told what the other brothers are thinking, briefly, but we are given no idea of what is in the daughter's mind. Here the withholding of point of view is used as a suspense device: the brothers, and a young doctor who joins them, all want to know what the daughter is going to do; indications are given that she has something unexpected in mind; some dissonant note is thus sounded which will be resolved later; the very fact that we are excluded from her thoughts evokes and increases this tension in the story. The daughter goes to her mother's graveside with flowers, and in a passage of exposition we enter her mind, historically, so to speak, learning how she felt about her family's fall in fortunes. The doctor observes her in the cemetery; she sees him watching. "Their eyes met." And in this extraordinary way, point of view switches to the doctor. With the doctor's eyes we watch the daughter walk down a hill in the twilight to a pond and walk into the pond, attempting suicide. We are with the doctor as he rescues her, experience with him the symbolic death of being under the dark water. He carries her back to the house and revives her. "She looked full into his face." And thereafter point of view switches back and forth between them, more and more rapidly, as they discover love for one another. More and more closely their thoughts are intertwined until, in the final sentence, point of view is marvelously, entirely mutually-held between them: " 'No, I want you, I want you,' was all he answered, blindly, with that terrible intonation which frightened her almost more than her horror lest he should *not* want her."

I don't for a minute suggest that Lawrence manipulated point of view consciously this way. I rather imagine he was pretty much totally unaware of it. Lawrence was not the master of technique that James was. What I am saying is that the dynamics of fiction, in the hands of a great writer, exert a control of their own, and that as a story comes closer finally to what it is really *about*, to "what happened" and who it is that it happened to, then the focusing power of point of view will narrow down accordingly. You can see this happen in any story you read, once you have learned to read this way.

And as far as the writer is concerned, we've seen that even when an author has misconceived his story, and attempted to tell it from the point of view of an unmoved character, he often finds that things begin to change on him. Despite the author's intentions, the point-of-view character will tend to occupy the center of his stage, and the interest and focus of his story will slip away from the character or characters he had originally intended to be central. "I'm wasting too much time just setting up this character who's seeing the story," the author may think to himself, if things aren't going well, or "My narrator's getting too interesting and throwing everything out of proportion."

But, if things do seem to be going well, he may just accept these new developments as an offering of the muse. "The story is changing to a new direction all on its own," he may say, or "The characters seem to be coming to life and taking over for themselves."

Mysteriously creative moments like these, experienced by most authors at one time or another, may just be the traditional and inevitable dynamics of fiction asserting themselves, a gradual triumph of technique over an initial misconception. It's in this sort of way that technique always liberates inspiration.

Monologues, and the Pathological First Person

Stories told in the monologue form would seem to be exceptions to our "rule" that the point-of-view character is the character moved by action or will become so. The monologist, after all, is presumed to be the same after he ends his harangue as he was before he began it. The monologist exists in a peculiar point of time. In regular first-person narration, the narrator tells of something that has happened to him that affected him, while in the monologue, the narrator simply reveals a state of mind: we can imagine him compulsively saying the same thing over and over. Monologues do in fact sometimes provide examples of exceptions to our rule—but for the most part it's endless examples of *unsuccessful* exceptions.

The monologue form, in all its versions, is probably the most awkward way to tell a story there is, and unfortunately beginning writers seem attracted to it unerringly. Even in the hands of an author skilled in dialogue or dialect, a monologue creates a very unsatisfactory story, and when used by a beginner it can make for very painful reading.

One basic trouble with the monologue form is that it disorients the reader. Who is it exactly that is talking? And then, is the reader being addressed directly? Or is a captive "visitor" there, in the barber chair or wherever, just somehow *listening*? Why is it the listener never *says* anything? And is the monologist anyway actually saying all this *out loud*? Or just thinking it to himself?

There are different kinds of monologues, with their own conventions and variations. There is the direct monologue, where the reader *is* being addressed directly. Then there is the dramatic monologue, in which a listener is supposedly or "actually" somehow there, between the monologist and the reader—an uneasy state of existence, to say the best of it. And there is the interior monologue, in which the narrator is not speaking aloud at all, but just somehow "thinking," either in complete sentences of in a sort of Freudian free association of fragmented thoughts, the "stream of consciousness" method more or less invented by James Joyce for Molly Bloom's "soliloquy" toward the end of *Ulysses*, and never used by anyone so well since, although it was once thought the method would revolutionize writing.

As passages in novels, monologues can certainly sometimes be vehicles for fine writing, just as the soliloquy can sometimes be brought alive on the stage with heightened writing. But one reason the soliloquies in drama *are* sometimes so beautiful is that dramatists realize how awkward and unreal the convention is and hence produce their absolute best to cover over the artificiality of the occasion. Where the soliloquy is useful, though, or perhaps even necessary in the theater, in order to establish motivation or characterization, or whatever, it is never really *necessary* in fiction, where the reader can easily be made privy to a character's thoughts or emotions in more straightforward, less "dramatic" ways. For a fiction writer to use the monologue form is to take up one of the play-wright's disadvantages for no necessary reason.

As far as telling a whole short story in the monologue is concerned, the disadvantages are terrible. There's the monotony of the single voice, for instance. Exposition's difficult, especially in the interior monologue, where the character is in the ridiculous position of saying or thinking, aloud to himself in some way, things he perfectly well knows he knows already. In many monologue stories, the character either fails to perceive the significance of the events he is describing, or has so different a reaction to them that the discrepancy between his reaction and the reader's is pretty much the whole intended effect of the story. In these cases, where the narrator is self-deceived, it often happens that he betrays himself "too early" and the alert reader grasps it all right away and then has to read on and on and on just to have it finally made obvious.

Some of us learned to dislike the monologue form early in life, with our first exposure, in high school, to that wretched poem of Robert Browning's, "My Last Duchess." It's entirely a monologue, the Duke looking up at a portrait of his last Duchess hanging up there on the wall, addressing some silent visitor-listener. As he runs on, he gradually reveals by his remarks about his pretty young wife, now dead of heartbreak or something, just what a coldhearted bastard he really is. He complains about how she smiled at everyone and everything, without regard to his situation in life, how she loved the flowers and cows in the fields just as much as she loved him, and so forth and so on, revealing himself unwittingly (as monologists often do) more and more as he goes on. Browning does more or less the same thing in another terrible poem in which one of the monks in a monastery complains about another: as the monologue develops, it becomes clear that the complaining monk is an awful fellow and the object of his hatred is a saint. Whatever the monologist is antagonistic to is invariably sentimentalized—the pathological narrator having stated the case against in such unfair and unperceptive terms that the reader is supposedly forced to sympathize with the object of his attack. (I've always felt, though, about "My Last Duchess" that the Duke had some cause for complaint: who wants a Duchess who cares as much about some cow out in the pasture as she does about you, and goes around simpering at the field hands all the time?)

Ring Lardner's famous monologue story, "Haircut," uses exactly the same method as "My Last Duchess," except he just flip-flopped it. Here the long-winded barber *admires* the practical joker he tells about; the reader is supposed to realize the joker is a sadist and hate him. (Actually, naturally, I always thought the fellow was fairly funny.) But the point I'm making remains the same. In most monologues we're supposed to perceive something entirely different from what we're being told; we're supposed to read between the lines exactly the opposite of what the lines say.

Why writers, expecially beginning writers, are continually attracted to this form is hard to see. Why would a writer want to tell a story from a point of view totally alien to him, from the point of view of a character whose every utterance must be designed secretly to convey the very opposite of what he's intending to say? The form violates rhetoric and denies the dynamics of fiction. Monologists in the pathological first person are presented as static: their attitudes toward the events of the story they describe are fixed, cannot be moved as a consequence of the action. This is a natural consequence, for in the pathological first person, the point-of-view figure is presented as being too warped or stupid for the events to have any effect on him. He won't even know what "happened" in the story, and, in fact, nothing has. Most monologues, then, are not really stories, but simply static character sketches of pathological types presented as imperceptive, unchanging first-person narrators. If the reason for writing such a monologue were to present a study of an unbalanced mind, then the interesting thing, surely, would be to show how the character got that way.

Too often in the monologue, all of the technique and most of the content are devoted only to establishing in the reader a different impression of the events of the story from the impression the narrator has of what he's telling. This is not only difficult to do—it puts the narrator and the reader in opposition to one another—but it scarcely seems worth doing, at least not just for its own sake. If carefully done, the resulting work can perhaps be considered something of a *tour de force,* but a *tour de force* is anyway only almost by definition just a matter of ability finally overcoming misconception.

Insofar as what's important ultimately, if it is simply this discrepancy between what the monologist (and/or perhaps the imagined "listener") realizes on the one hand, and what the reader is intended to realize on the other, then the final effect achieved is indeed one of irony—but of a kind of irony established simply for its own sake and no other purpose.

Irony and Point of View

Irony is ultimately an aspect of *tone,* the author's attitude or voice in the story. But in important ways irony is involved in aspects of plot and character, ultimately also no doubt as a result of what the author "feels" about the story, but not seeming to be so—at least, not so directly. The fiction writer, playing God with his characters and their stories, can create tricks of plotting, ironic "turns of event," that resemble the "tricks of Fate" that we speak of as being "ironic" in everyday life.

Thus, one way the tone of irony is made manifest in fiction is by what it is that is made to happen to the characters. The plot itself achieves the irony, or seems to. And, again, this is akin to irony in life. There is a certain irony, for instance, in the fact that the astronaut John Glenn injured himself by slipping in the bathtub. Why is that? Well, to spell it out, it is because after surviving all the perils of orbiting the earth, he came to grief in the most mundane of ways. Closely akin to this is the idea of "poetic justice": as when a man who makes faulty bathtubs is injured in one himself. His punishment somehow ironically "fits" (is appropriate to) the crime. "Irony of Fate" of this sort comes about through the fact of what happened being either singularly appropriate, as in the case of the bathtub manufacturer, or singularly inappropriate, as in the case of John Glenn. In each case there seems to be an ironic relation between the man and the man's fate, as if there were a mocking attitude behind what has happened, as if someone were laughing somewhere. In both cases, the singularly appropriate and the singularly inappropriate, it seems as if there were some controlling force—Fate, or God, or simply "events"—that somehow *arranged* things in this mockingly singular way. There is not necessarily an indication that justice has been done; what is involved may be (in fact often is) the very *opposite* of justice. A mocking attitude is what's common to all forms of irony, whether it be the "tragic" or "dramatic" irony of fate or the facetious ironic tone of satire.

The mocking effect derives from an element of dissimulation, a pretense of ignorance, which is basic to the techniques of irony. "Socratic irony," for instance, is the method of feigning ignorance so as to confute an opponent in debate. The word "irony" itself comes from the Greek *eirōn,* a stock character in early Greek comedy who always put down the boastful *alazon* by using sly understatement and concealing his knowledge.

Thus irony is often said to be composed of "two separate views, one superimposed on the other." What's meant here is that a naïve, uninformed, excluded point of view is contrasted with a point of view that is sophisticated, informed, included. Perhaps it would be simpler to say that differing degrees of knowingness are confronted.

These two contrasted points of view can be seen,

for instance, in ironic speech, which is often close to sarcasm. One man tells a joke and the other man says, "That was really funny." Now if the comment is sincere, it doesn't concern us. If it was sarcastic, both men will know that it wasn't sincere. If the remark was ironic, the man who made it will know it wasn't sincere, but the fellow who told the joke won't know, or at least won't be sure, although others who may be listening to them will. These are the differing degrees of knowingness confronted, and it is how irony is created.

Irony is a tone. In conversation, it may be a tone of voice. In fiction, it is the tone of the author's voice.

It's in this way, for instance, that a rather monotonous tone of irony is created in stories told in the monologue form by a self-deceived narrator. The author and the reader supposedly share a knowledge that the monologist doesn't have: reader and author enjoy a superiority at the point-of-view character's expense. But used in more promising forms than the monologue, the techniques of irony are capable of both the most powerful and most subtle effects.

When irony is achieved through the aspects of plot and character, rather than through the aspects of tone and style and point of view and mood, it is referred to as "dramatic irony." Dramatic irony is situational; it is usually achieved, "set up," in the course of the narrative, then finally resolved. And dramatic irony is used for both comic and tragic effects. Comic dramatic irony is easily demonstrated in stage plays, as when a man boasts how faithful his wife is, and we the audience know that her lover is under the bed. Satiric irony requires our collaboration: we must share the attitude of mockery that the author is presumed to have toward his characters. The author and reader discern that the characters are funny or fatuous or fashionable or futile or whatever. The characters in satire have a different view of their actions, however: to themselves they are serious, sensible, sincere, and so on. When we resist the irony, when we are made to feel by the author a greater compassion for the characters and their situation than the author appears to be showing himself (either in his tone or in his working of the developments of the plot), then this can become tragic irony—at least when it is sublimely and dramatically achieved.

In old-fashioned fiction, it was relatively easy to detect the author's tone; often in the omniscient-author point-of-view method he would obtrude his presence and make his comments on the action directly. The commentary might be ironic in tone, but more likely it was sentimental or didactic. In contemporary fiction, the author is often conspicuously absent—especially in the first-person and central-intelligence point-of-view methods. It is often now far more difficult to decide just what an author feels about his characters and their goings-on.

Thus the older-fashioned methods tended toward clarity and sympathy—a kind of subjectivity on the author's part that made for a feeling of involvement. The newer-fashioned methods tend toward ambiguity and irony—a kind of objectivity on the author's part that makes for a feeling of detachment.

Setting

Setting is often described as "the element of place or location in fiction"—*locale* was the old-fashioned word for it. But setting implies location in time, time of day as well as historic time, and such matters as the weather out of doors or the temperature in the room where it all happens—all of these factors are customarily included in the term "setting." It may seem of small consequence, and in stories where the setting doesn't matter, it *is* of small consequence. But in successful stories, where everything works together, it's useful to see what choice of setting contributes. With a writer like Hemingway, for instance, who seemed to have a choice of milieu for his stories—Spain, Africa, upstate Michigan, and so on—one could easily think through why each story is set wherever it is. Putting aside biographical considerations, one sees that it is the perfect setting chosen, and that it contributes to the whole successful unity of the story.

As with all other aspects of a successful story, the setting may be basic to the original conception or may be the result of conscious and deliberate choice in the course of composition. If it is a question of choice, then the first decision about setting for any author—especially the author of a short story, where economy is always at such a premium—is the selection of the place itself, for here he can make use of certain attributes of his setting that already exist either actually in the place itself, or can be presumed to exist in the reader's conception of the place, without having to create these connotations himself.

One notices this best if he has the occasion to consider a number of stories by different authors all about the same place—as, for instance, in preparing an anthology of stories about New York City. Virtually every American writer has written a New York City story—Melville, Crane, James, Fitzgerald, Wharton, Wolfe, and Malamud, Cheever, and James Baldwin, and so on—and it is fascinating to see how the single similar element, setting, functions in each in a different successful way. You could do the same with a group of stories about "the sea" or "Paris" or "farm life" or "the South" or "suburbia" or whatever. I put each of these locales in quotation marks, for it is their connotations as much as their actuality that is put to work in fiction.

In the case of New York City, for instance, it is clearly a place about which certain generalizations can be made—whether they are inaccurate clichés or even contradictory is not important—and this makes the city useful and effective as a setting for an apparently limitless variety of situations and themes. In terms of plot and character, there is so much mobility in the city, both upward and downward, that it is an appropriate setting for any character's quick rise or fall. Because the city has more people of all social classes in close-crowded conjunction, it is an appropriate setting for any odd encounter—as between an actress and a bum, between a playboy and a secretary—with corresponding opportunities for depicting the injustices of social distinction and the extremes of poverty and wealth. New York City is between America and Europe and hence is a likely scene for conflict between the two. There are, in fact, so many comings and goings of all sorts in New York that an author can make virtually any plot or characterization plausible.

Many of the traditional themes of fiction—the corrupting powers of ambition, the nature of one's responsibility to self and to others, the tragedy of loneliness, the paradoxes and ambiguities of compromise—all seem congenial to the city's qualities—its crowded loneliness, its veneration for the new, its bustling immorality, its commercialism, its sense of busy pointlessness. The city is available as a symbol of opportunity and freedom and success, and of the empty underside of these qualities. Useful as these connotations of New York have been to many writers, however, it would be absurd to set a story there, rather than some place that is better known to the author, if that place would function as well in his story.

Conrad used the sea, Faulkner used the South, Cheever used suburbia, and in so doing, these authors managed to create, from story to story and from novel to novel, a world with connotations not just of the place itself, but from their own individual perception and creation of it. Setting can work this way: there can be a vaulable reinforcement back from the depicted "world." Hardy's "Wessex" takes on connotations from book to book that the actual Dorset or West Country never suggest in themselves, and the same is of course true of Cheever's "Shady Hill" and Faulkner's "Yoknapatawpha." The beginning writer, however, experimenting, ought not to expect any virtue as such from what's disparagingly called "regionalism." What he should concern himself with is how the setting of each story enhances it, or can be made to do so.

This is as likely to be achieved by description of place as it is by choice of place. "Description" has been given a bad reputation by bad writers. Reading Sir Walter Scott, you'd skip the "description"—he'd imprison a heroine and then describe the castle for two pages, how and when and whyfore it was built, and what of, stone by boring stone. It was description for description's sake, or for "verisimilitude" or "historical accuracy" or something. It had no integral part, no function in the narrative, and one was right to skip it. This is not true of a passage of description in Thomas Hardy or any other good writer, where the description contributes to the whole work symbolically or emotionally—enhancing in a variety of ways that can be demonstrated.

"Passages" of description, as such, seldom appear in today's fiction, at least not long ones. But whatever description is provided can be analyzed, can be shown to be "loaded" or "slanted" or "colored" in such a way as to achieve an effect. The language can be effectively freighted (with adjectives or adverbs that are dolorous or cheerful or whatever); details of the place described can be selected or omitted depending on the sort of effect desired; or the point-of-view character can be made to view the setting with an attitude which suitably colors the description of it. There are these and all sorts of other ways in which an author can render the setting so as to create a desired effect.

In fact, it is an instructive exercise for a beginning writer to put himself to: to describe the exact same place—a room or a garden or a city street—in two ways, first as forbidding, say, then as attractive, without changing many of the actual details.

But that is, of course, simply an exercise. What matters is to render the setting of a specific story exactly so it perfectly enhances all the other aspects of that story. A passage of description should foreshadow action for the reader, whether symbolically or otherwise; the perception of the setting should help delineate character, whether of the point-of-view character or otherwise. Henry James, speaking of the artificiality of separating "parts" of fiction, said he could not "conceive a passage of description that is not in its intention narrative, nor a passage of dialogue that is not in its intention descriptive." Thus the setting must contribute to the other aspects of the story, as well as to the whole.

Style

There is a way of thinking about fiction that maintains that "style" could be at the heart of the whole matter, just as there's the simpler-minded thought that *plot* is the whole thing, or *character*. We've quoted Lubbock as saying that it was *point of view* that "governed" method in the craft of fiction. It could equally be said that the all-important thing is *theme*, or *tone*, or virtually any other aspect of the techniques of fiction.

It is the inseparability of part from part, and part from whole, in a successful work of fiction that makes this shift in emphasis not just possible but plausible. You can look at a successful short story from any angle, come in on it in one direction, and maintain that it was that facet that made the whole thing shine so. To maintain that style rules all, however, is to make the word stand for more than it normally needs to.

Theme usually refers to the element of meaning in a work of fiction: what the story "says," insofar as it is paraphrasable. *Tone* is the customary word for the element of the author's presence in the work: his attitude toward it, say, insofar as that is detectable. And *style* usually is confined to mean the element of language: words, syntax, punctuation, and so on—everything from the simple mechanics to the rhetoric that may reflect a given author's originality of utterance. To some extent, obviously, theme and tone and style—as well as "voice" and "vision" and "world view" and so on—all overlap one another so much in meaning that they can be thought of as all meaning pretty much the same thing. It's a short step from that realization to taking one word of your own choice or devising and just saying that it *does* represent the whole thing.

But even if "style" is limited strictly to elements of the author's language it is still a most significant aspect of fiction technique. There are many, many things involved. Word usage itself is just the first: style will differ if long, "difficult," scholarly or elegant words and terms are used, instead of short, colloquial, "ordinary" words of everyday speech. Similarly, the lengths and constructions of sentences will have an effect: one thinks of the effective difference between, say, the long, convoluted, intricate, complex, tortuous sentences of Henry James that seem to hang forever before banging-in at the end, and the curt sentences of Hemingway. It's not just a question of an older style of writing; Hemingway's contemporary, Faulkner, constantly uses those paragraph-long sentences, full of negative-dependent qualifying clauses— "not because" this and "not because of" that—evoking as he pretends to put aside. Certainly it would be possible both to underestimate and to overestimate the importance of sentence construction to the very different worlds that Hemingway and James are creating in their fiction. What should not be overlooked is how exactly appropriate is the style to the whole in the case of each of them, and in fact in the case of any successful writer.

Nor is it of course simply sentence structure that achieves this appropriateness of style. There's the matter of verb tenses: the use of conditional forms, and the use of past and present tense. The effect of various grammatical mechanics will contribute: as, for instance, differences in punctuation, such as setting off parenthetical matter in dashes, or commas, or whatever. Paragraphing and italics and exclamation points must matter; essayists use the semicolon all the time, yet it virtually never appears in fiction; there must be a reason. And there is the whole business of dialogue—not just how much it is used, but the cadences of it. For surely a great part of what is called a writer's "vision" comes from how he listens.

A writer's style reflects the world he perceives and helps to create the world he depicts. The Jamesian world is more elegant, elaborate, intricate, and complex than the Hemingway world, and the Jamesian language reflects and depicts it as such. But "style," as we have used the word, is only one aspect of fiction technique; it contributes only as it works with the other aspects of fiction.

The interconnections are throughout, as always. The aspect of point of view will have a determining effect on style, and be determined by it: whoever is seeing or telling the story must see and talk in a way that works with all the rest. This, of course, brings us to the aspect of characterization: the sorts of characters the author creates will speak the language of his world. What "happens" to them, the plots of his stories, will be the sorts of things that happen to those sorts of characters in that sort of place—wherever it is or whatever it's like there—for the setting, too, will be determined by its relation to all the other aspects of the author's world.

What we have said of the successful short story—that everything in it must somehow work with everything else—seems to be the case too with the inseparable mixture of compatible aspects that somehow create the recognizable individual "world" of each of the major writers' whole body of work down through his career.

Theme

A writer, of course, is God in relation to the world he creates and is responsible not only for every sparrow's fall—for each character's fate—but is also responsible for the coherence of his world as a whole. This coher-

ence in the world he creates is constituted of two concepts he holds, which may be in conflict: one is his
world view, his sense of the way the world is; and the
other is his sense of morality, his sense of the way the
world ought to be.

In some writers, the sense of morality predominates.
Thus, it seems to me, Tolstoi, Dostoyevski, James,
Jane Austen, George Eliot, and Conrad, for instance,
are writers who impose their own high code of right
and wrong on the characters of their creation, "punishing" the characters' transgressions (which are of
course also of the writer's own creation) with a
Jehovah-like impartiality and harshness. In some other
writers, the world view predominates. Thus, Melville,
Dreiser, Hemingway, Faulkner, and Hardy, for instance, seem to me to be writers who impose their
dark sense of the way the world is on their characters,
"punishing" them not out of any sense of the rightness
or wrongness of their acts, but rather according to the
immutable laws of the world as they see it. The "punishment" meted out to two adulterous heroines may
serve as an example: Anna Karenina suffers because
Tolstoi is convinced of the immortality of her actions;
Tess D'Urberville is sentenced by Hardy's conviction
that the world "order" is cruelly indifferent and random.

This distinction has some nice parallels—one is to a
traditional dual role ascribed to art: to imitate life on
the one hand, and to instruct on the other. Another
parallel is to the role ascribed to God Himself: He has
created this world and the people in it and all the
things they do, good and evil, but He too seems torn
between a sense of the way things ought to be and the
way they are. Sympathy for the characters He created
doesn't seem to enter into it all that much; for, except
in the case of a miracle (which bears the same relation to life that the *deus ex machina* solution bears to
literature—that is, it is a fault in the plotting), divine
intervention is withheld, and the world is left to run
pretty much by itself.

In literature, the same is true. The writer's sense of
the coherence of the world he has created is greater

than any sympathy he may feel for the characters he has created. He has (and yet has not, in some strange way) the power to alter his characters' fate. How willful the great writers sometimes seem! Who has not wished that Hardy would let Tess and Angel have a bit of happiness at the end? Who hasn't wished that James would release Lambert Strether or Isabel Archer from their fine Jamesian conscience? Wished happiness and a large family to André and Natasha?

In this foolish "wishing," the effects of the novel are a bit different from those of the drama. It would seem ludicrous to wish for Oedipus an escape from his own self-condemnation, or to wish Lear a happy old age bouncing Cordelia's babies on his knee. Part of the difference is in the stature and rigidity of the tragic figures; part of it is the way the authors of the great tragedies limit any sense of alternative to the characters themselves and never let the audience lose the sense of the inevitability of the catastrophe.

Fiction, on the other hand, commonly brings us closer to the characters, who are in the first place people more approachable, more like us; and their fate is less symbolically ours (as in drama) than it is somehow *actually* ours, through that "wishing" involvement that anyone who has ever been engrossed by a novel must admit having experienced. To wish in this way for a "happy" outcome for the characters, when the author has prepared the book's coherence to demand their suffering, is of course to wish for the story to be spoiled, to wish for literature to become popular novel. The author deliberately makes us want for the characters what we know cannot be, what we know even ought not be. The novelist is constantly provoking in the reader the sense that "things might have been different" if only some twist or turn in the plot might have allowed it, or if the protagonist (or even some secondary character) might only have relented a little. The effect is a wrench on our sympathies—and we feel either a resentment (perhaps at first) that makes us ask, "Why did it have to be so?" or an acceptance (perhaps finally) that makes us say, "Yes, it had to be so," and then ponder the reasons. In either case, we readers turn back to the book for the reasons or answers.

A book of this sort, when the last page is read, is not "finished." We have a sense of there being—or of there having been (it's nothing less than the metaphysics of the matter that's confusing tenses here)—*more* somehow. This *more* is sometimes spoken of as the book's "values," or its "meaning," or what the book "has to say." The most useful word, probably, is "theme." Clearly this overlaps with what we have been speaking of as the book's "world"—its imitation of the real world as colored and refracted by the author's sense of its coherence, the "order" that the author has made from the chaos that is real life.

Thus it is that the fiction writer's method, in order to turn our attention to what it is he "has to say" about how the world is or ought to be, is deliberately to create in the reader suspense, involvement, and a developing understanding of and hence sympathy with the characters he created; and yet to be himself, finally, above that sympathy and, like God, ruthlessly true to the coherence of the world he has created, true to his theme.

When we speak of the "world" of a great book like *Middlemarch,* we mean more than just the sociological world of shopkeepers, gentry, and professional men that George Eliot depicted. When we speak of the "world" of *Moby Dick,* we mean more than just the microcosm of the ship. We include in this the cosmic view *and* the ethical attitudes of the author who created it. Each great book will have a "world," but in those cases where we have several works by the same author and there is a degree of continuity between them, we have come to speak easily of the *author's* world. Thus, "the world of Dickens," "the world of F. Scott Fitzgerald," or "Hemingway's world." With Fitzgerald we mean more than just a world of richish people who drink too much—we mean a world where outcome depends on Fitzgerald's own sense of right and wrong and his sense of how the world works. It is *the* world, our world, everyone's world, seen through

Fitzgerald's ethic as well as his eyes—as seen by (or through) his *self*. Hemingway's world is not just bull-fighters and big game hunters worried about their bravery, it is a world in which "values" exist—even if they seem to consist in nothing more than an inside code of okay stoical behavior. These values in literature do not accumulate—literature is not philosophy—and may even be contradictory. One imagines, for instance, that what Henry James would consider "good" or "bad" behavior, Hemingway would consider to be fussy distinctions, and one is quite certain that James would consider Hemingway's self-testing heroes quite foolish. What matters is not what the values and themes are, but rather how they are integrated into the work. As Norman Mailer says of Hemingway, and of D. H. Lawrence and Henry Miller and other such writers: "Everything they wrote was part of one continuing book—the book of their life and the vision of their existence."

James Joyce spoke of the necessity for the artist to be wholly removed from his narrative, "behind or above his handiwork, invisible, refined out of existence, indifferent, paring his fingernails." There is no real inconsistency here. The world Joyce created in his fictions (in *Dubliners, Portrait,* and *Ulysses*) is a world he created, after all. It was chosen by him, redrawn by him, colored by him; the characters speak and think in Joyce's language, and though it is made not to seem so, they do what he bids them. If he has "refined himself out of existence" in it, is it not still nevertheless his world?

"Theme" and "world view" as an aspect of fiction seem to come very much after the fact. A beginning short story writer will have very little sense of any overall coherence in his efforts so far, and it's better that he doesn't. But any editor or writing instructor who has read three or four first stories by a new writer may very well be able to find (if he but pause a few moments to consider them) a connective thread in the stories—whether in situation, milieu, characterization, or wherever. There is a special kind of thing the writer's doing, a kind of special way he has of looking at things, a kind of special thing that he sees, a kind of special cadence or odd conjunction in his writing—something about it that is just not standard or ordinary. This potential new vision-world-voice must certainly be an aspect of the work worth encouraging.

And it may seem, too, that the short story provides less room for the flexing of self and vision-world-voice than does the novel. To some extent this is true. But there is no limit on the "size" of theme or subject, as such, in a short story. Any "limitations" are clearly not on the story's content, but on the author's self-expression. And excellence in art seems finally to be determined not by the extent the author expresses himself, but by the fineness of the created work, judged independently of the author.

The Short Story and the New Criticism

Certainly the American short story is not today as popular and vital a form as it was in the 1920s and 1930s, when Scribner's would alternate a novel by Hemingway, Fitzgerald, or Wolfe with a volume of short stories by the same author, or when Faulkner, Sherwood Anderson, Eudora Welty, Katherine Anne Porter, and all the others were writing the short story masterpieces that now appear in our college textbook anthologies. In the 1950s, the short story seemed to be having a sort of renaissance in the little magazines and literary quarterlies, in the hands of such authors as Saul Bellow, Philip Roth, Thomas Pynchon, John Barth, and dozens of others; but they've all gone over to novel writing now. Short stories by major writers—genuine short stories that aren't excerpts adapted from novels-in-progress—are really very rare these days.

There are some interlocking vicious circles in commercial publishing that seem to explain what's happened to the short story. Magazine editors say they don't publish stories because the good writers don't write them; good writers say they don't write them because the magazine market's gone. Book publishers won't do collections of a writer's short stories because they sell even worse than novels—"After you've done a novel," they say, "then maybe we'll consider a book of stories"—yet they complain that most first novels they see lack craft and maturity. *And* yet, when a writer *is* established and "mature," chances are he's entirely given over writing short stories. "I just don't seem to think in terms of short stories anymore," he may say, thinking of them as just "finger exercises" for his "bigger" and "more important" work in the novel form. You could go round and round forever, debating which came first: no good short stories, or the lack of a market for them.

The various commercial "market" reasons don't seem to add up to a whole answer. If a major writer were to do a short story, for instance, surely he'd place it instantly, at one or another of the admittedly few national magazines that still do fiction. But anyway, serious literary writers don't write for *markets*. They don't aim their "material" at "outlets" in the one-to-one way commercial writers do. Even most of their *novels* aren't aimed at the big, popular, mass bestseller market. And very few of the masterpieces of the golden age of the American short story appeared in the high-paying, slick weekly magazines whose "demise" is so lamented by those who explain the lack of short stories by saying "the market's just not there."

The real reason the short story seems so uncongenial now may well lie with the form itself: because of the very excellence and intricacy the short story achieved, it may perhaps have become at once too limiting and also too demanding—on readers and writers alike. Modern readers feel that a story fails to "move" them or "involve" them the way a novel does. Modern writers feel that they can't "say all they have to say" or "express" themselves in a short story the way they can in a novel or a piece of personal journalism. The irony is, that the American short story evolved in an aesthetic that denied the validity of both these complaints, an aesthetic that considered a work of literary art as more or less an independent *object*, and denied the relevance of its effectiveness as either an *expression* of the author or a *communication* to the reader.

This aesthetic was the so-called "New Criticism." It represented the main way literature was taught and thought about from the 1930s through the 1950s. Some feel that the intensive "internal analysis" methods of this school of criticism were developed to cope with the rich complexities of the fiction written after World War One. Others invidiously imply that the opposite was true: that much modern fiction was made deliberately ambiguous and intricate so as to be able to yield its meanings and subtleties only to the detailed readings and ingenious explications of the New Critic. At any rate, modern writing and modern criticism seemed made for one another. The short story, as a form, "yielded" to the New Criticism especially well.

The New Criticism in its purest form aggressively considered art as *object*, and certain advantages and implications devolve from this. The really nifty questions in aesthetics—like "If a copy of *Hamlet* and a copy of a dreadful mystery novel are both on a desert island with no one to read them, is one still a better book than the other?" or James Joyce's "If a man hacking in anger at a piece of wood by accident carves out the image of a cow, can it be a work of art?"—all such metaphysical questions ultimately relate to the effect on the appreciator or to the intention of the creator in regard to an *object* of art.

To consider the effect on the appreciator of the object as being the relevant question is to consider the story as a communication, which it is certainly possible to do. The only trouble is, this eventually leads to a vote-taking kind of aesthetic, bringing up questions like: how many people liked the story how much, and how qualified were they as readers, and so on. It all leads *away* from the story.

Popularity doesn't seem to mean much, one way or the other. Northrop Frye has a useful example to show there is no correlation, either direct or inverse, between the merit of art and the degree of public response to it: "Shakespeare was more popular than Webster, but not because he was a better dramatist; Keats was less popular than Montgomery, but not because he was a better poet." Frye goes on to say that "whatever popularity Shakespeare and Keats have *now* is equally the result of the publicity of criticism." By "the publicity of criticism" he means the cumulative effect, down through the centuries, of reading literature *as* literature, considering art *as* art, instead of thinking of it as something else, as communication or expression.

If you consider art as expression, then the relevant questions have to do with the intention of the creator, how the work of art relates to his life and thought, and to the period in which it was created, and so on. Again, these questions tend to lead away from the story, or did, in the obsessive "historical-biographical" way they were pursued prior to the introduction of the New Criticism. Considering art primarily as an expression of the artist was called "the intentional fallacy" by New Critics; as considering it as communication was called "the affective fallacy."

So, but, if the only non-fallacious way to consider art is as object, the problem remains of demonstrating what is good, apart from the testimony of both reader and writer. This brings up objective qualities, as for instance, "unity," a quality which may be difficult (although actually not impossible) to demonstrate in some works (a Gothic cathedral, for instance, or Shakespeare's *Antony and Cleopatra*), but is certainly easily demonstrated in most well-wrought short stories. The short story as a form benefits especially from this sort of objective consideration; poetry and novels seem so much more direct communications of emotions to the reader, more effusive expressions of the author.

Similarly, the short story yields well to the influential critical precepts of James Joyce, the Joycean aesthetics being a sort of romantic precursor of the academic New Criticism—so romantic, in fact, in the high-flying way Joyce has Stephen present them in *Portrait of the Artist*, that some doubt how seriously they are to be taken.

In *Portrait*, Stephen flamboyantly interprets the three qualities Aquinas had said were necessary for art: *integritas, consonantia,* and *claritas*. The first he translates as "wholeness," by which he means the identity or separateness of the art object from the rest of the universe—thus it is to be considered apart from the perceiver and the creator. *Consonantia,* or "harmony," is the second requirement of art: "led by its formal lines, you apprehend it as balanced part against part within its limits . . . You apprehend it as complex, multiple, divisible, separable, made up of its parts, the result of its parts and their sum, harmonious." *Claritas,* which Stephen translates as "radiance," is the "luminous silent stasis of esthetic pleasure" which is "called forth, prolonged, and at last resolved" by what Stephen calls "the rhythm of beauty": the "esthetic relation of part to part in any esthetic whole, or of an esthetic whole to its part or parts or any part to the esthetic whole of which it is a part."

Consideration of the relationship of parts to part, and of parts to whole, seems really, finally, the most reliable way to demonstrate the excellence of a work of art. A short story, for instance, considered as an object separate from the author and his intentions and separate from the reader and his reactions, is to be evaluated according to internal relationships, not external ones.

This is not to say that one judges a story by the jigsaw-puzzle ingenuity by which its parts are fitted to make its whole. A story is not constructed as a "pre-established design" to which all else is jointed. And no special premium is put on complexity of interrelationships between aspects of the story. The greatest literary works—*Hamlet, Middlemarch,* a first-rate story by Eudora Welty or Sherwood Anderson—will certainly have complexity. But I'm sure that there's also a lot of bad art with a great deal of complexity. A "simple" story may have a great fineness of construction that secures its excellence. The matter is not quantitative. Excellence depends on the kind of the interrelationships, on the "harmony" and effectiveness of them—not on their number. The interrelationships are to be analyzed, not counted.

The assumption is, then, that excellence in fiction, or its opposite, can be demonstrated. Imagine that a reader has been pleased by a story, and since it pleased him he feels that "hence" it is a *good* story. This experience and conclusion are open to proof or disproof, depending on the reader and story. If the reader was pleased by a bad story, it is possible to show him why it was bad, if he's willing to listen—which your average reader pleased by a bad story is unlikely to be. If he is pleased by a good story, it is equally possible to prove to him that it was in fact good, and show him why it was good. This can be done only by showing him how harmoniously and effectively the parts of the story work together so as to create the story's excellence.

By the careful reading and minute analysis which was characteristic of the New Criticism, every part can be shown to work with every other part in a successful short story. The parts are so interwrought that they are truly inseparable, and the seeming artificiality in the practice of separating the parts from one another and from the whole to discuss them, the theoretical impossibility of so doing, is just that: artificial and impossible. But to demonstrate the excellence of a story, one demonstrates *not* the separability of the aspects, but their very inseparability.

We've already quoted Henry James on the way each aspect of fiction will serve several purposes. "People often talk of these things," he complains, "as if they had a kind of internecine distinctness, instead of melting into each other at every breath, and being intimately associated parts of one general effort of expression." Then James goes on to say, in a famous passage:

> A novel is a living thing, all one and continuous,
> like any other organism, and in proportion as it
> lives will it be found, I think, that in each of the
> parts there is something of each of the other parts.

What James says here the novel is true especially of the novels *he* wrote, which have a complex unity and a close relation between part and whole. It is not necessarily true of all good novels. The novel since Cervantes, Fielding, and Stern, and despite and after James and Joyce, has been an indulgent, open form, permissive to the digression, the ramble, the airing of "ideas"—the form in which (except for the essay) the literary artist can most directly "express" himself. But what James says, is *necessarily* true of the short story form. There is no role in it, indeed no *room* in it, for material that doesn't contribute "directly or indirectly," as Poe said, to the work's "single and unique effect" or—to use a more sophisticated term of the New Criticism—to the work's "whole actual meaning." And it is this necessity for what James called an organic unity that made the short story, in terms of the New Criticism's aesthetic theory, virtually the loftiest of literary forms.

But it is an aesthetically ascetic form, very demanding on both writer and reader. The modern short story requires a disciplining of technique and a refining of self out of the work that contemporary writers neither feel that they want nor recognize that they need. And while it demands this detachment of self from the writer, the story makes equal demands for the reader's detachment from his own emotions. No reader can pick up a short story and expect to "submerge" himself in it for a long lonely evening, much less a rainy weekend. No writer can expect to celebrate his friends, destroy his enemies, push his predelictions and prejudices, air his grievances, propound his theories of sociology or psychology or politics or religion or whatever—*all* in one short story. That's for the novel to do.

Too much, though, has been asked of the novel over the years. There has always been the myth of The

Great American Novel that was finally going to show us to ourselves and save us from ourselves. It was somehow going to be our salvation. That myth, and its mystique, have faded somewhat now, and it's just as well, for it's based in an aesthetic that exalts art falsely. It all leads eventually into the same blind alley Tolstoi went to the very end of in *What Is Art?*, where he deduced that since what's virtuous in human acts are those which promote the brotherhood of man, then that art is best which most promotes the brotherhood of man—hence he concludes with the greatness of *Uncle Tom's Cabin*. This is what comes of asking art to be something other than art.

The reason James Joyce emphasized the "luminous silent *stasis* of esthetic pleasure" was to distinguish true art from the false *kinetic* arts of pornography and didacticism, which ask of art what art should not do—whether it is "more" or "less" does not matter. It's why the textbooks of the New Criticism insisted that students be taught to read a poem *as a poem*, and not as anything else. What we've looked for in the Great American Novel over the years, however wrongly—that it come to "save" us, or whatever—is something that no one in his right mind would ask of the Great American Short Story. The artistic demands of the form itself are too great for us to ask more than just that they be met.

Many of today's novelists, possibly as a result of a misreading or misunderstanding of the apparently one-to-one identification of the man's life and the man's work in the cases of such admired recent writers as Hemingway and Fitzgerald, have lost the ability to distinguish between their troubled selves and their troubled times on the one hand, and their writing on the other. The American writer now, far from being "behind or above his handiwork," as Joyce wanted him to be, "indifferent, paring his fingernails," is now publicly biting his nails all through his novels and nonfiction. The short story is not susceptible to such indulgence, but the personal-polemical magazine article of course *is*. That's why so many of our literary writers have turned to it as a respite between their long novels. But far from disciplining the techniques blunted by the permissive, freewheeling novel form, the article just further indulges the novelistic excesses.

Fiction and the New Journalism

It's sometimes said these days that journalism may be the contemporary literary art: that the nonfiction book of reportage is replacing the novel; that the magazine article is replacing the short story. The argument is aesthetically ridiculous, of course, but not insupportable in other ways.

Certainly it's true, for instance, that nonfiction books outsell all but the sleaziest best-seller novels, and that nonfiction is published ten-to-one more than fiction, when it used to be just about the other way. Fiction doesn't "sell"—it doesn't sell books *or* magazines.

What can one say about the decline in the popularity of fiction? One can say it's due to the new nonfiction taking over its function of telling us about ourselves, or that it's due to the crass commercialism of the establishmentarian publishing companies, or due to the death of the popular magazines that once published short stories, or due to the substitute entertainment-and-escape provided by TV, or due to a change in the nation's leisure habits—everyone having stopped reading and gone to play tennis. One can say that it's contemporary fiction's own fault, for being so negative or inaccessible or interior, or whatever. Or, one can deny that there's been much decline at all: one can say that, after all, serious literary fiction never was read much anyway. There really isn't anything more one can say about this, and it doesn't matter much anyway, the decline in popularity doesn't, or

148

shouldn't; for good writers should go on writing good fiction whether it's popular or not.

But good writers have alimony and egos. A lot of good writers—many of them originally fiction writers—have turned to journalism, tempted by the money, readership, and influence promised them by book and magazine editors. And there has evolved as a result a sort of reportage—referred to as "the New Journalism" when it first appeared—which is often so personal and subjective, often so original in style and approach, that it very nearly does seem like a new art form.

But of course journalism is not fiction, and it's not going to replace fiction because it does something fiction doesn't do, and it doesn't do what fiction does. The New Journalism certainly uses some of the superficial methods of fiction—direct dialogue, scene-setting, use of participant narrator point of view, and in some recent cases even attempts to render some of the depicted character's "thoughts." But the basic methods of fiction—such essential processes of creation as those we might call "distillation," "dramatization," and "distortion," for instance—are precluded to even the most imaginative journalism.

Distillation, or whatever else you choose to call the process by which the fiction writer abstracts from the general reality he perceives so as to create the specific imagined reality of his work, is a process of transformation; as such, it has nothing to do with the journalist's transcription of actual reality, no matter how insightful the facts the journalist observes or how significant the details he records.

Dramatization, just one name for the process by which the imagination of the fiction writer engages the imagination of the reader, is the method of making something happen in a story, of showing character affected by action in a crucial way; and it has nothing to do with even the most vivid effects of the New Journalism, as when it "dramatizes" a day in the life of a movie star, or "renders" a sporting event, or "brings alive" a political convention.

Distortion, perhaps not the best word to describe the fiction writer's creation of a depicted rather than an actual reality, is like the painter's process of giving a true sense of dimension by falsely emphasizing depths and shadows, of subtly exaggerating according to his unique vision. Such artistic distortion in literature has no more to do with even the least objective techniques of journalism than the emotion of an Expressionist painting has to do with the flat-light "accuracy" of a newspaper photograph.

It is the element of imagination that is, or ought to be, present in fiction, just as imagination is not present in journalism, or certainly ought not to be. Fiction and journalism will ultimately simply not mix, although certain recent popular books show how indistinct the line between them is getting to be.

Truman Capote's *In Cold Blood*, which he called "a nonfiction novel," used fiction methods for a completely factual account of a murder; his *Answered Prayers*, a novel of high society, mixes real names with fictional names, but Capote claims every event is actual. E. L. Doctorow's best seller, *Ragtime*, mixed actual historical characters in actual historical event with actual historical characters in imagined event, plus purely imaginary characters and events. Robert Coover's *The Public Burning of Julius and Ethel Rosenberg*, published after *Ragtime* but conceived earlier, uses similar methods; there is simultaneity of invention in the air. Gay Talese's *Honor Thy Father* told of an actual Mafia family factually, but presumed to render a depicted character's "thoughts"— presumably not as imagined or projected by Talese, but as recalled by the character, recounted to Talese, and simply inserted into the narrative as fact.

These books are interesting as experiments, clearly; but they make for an uncertain reading experience. In the case of the fictionalized nonfiction, one tends to wonder how some intimate "fact" could possibly be verified by the reporter. In the case of the nonfictionalized fiction, one gets to wondering about which of it all is "actual" and who the "real-life" characters are. The mixed form doesn't seem to make for a greater reality or conviction, just for uncertainty—a lot of guessing and doubt.

Despite the continuing decline in the popularity of straightforward fiction, people seldom speak these days, as they did a few years back, of the "death" of the novel or the short story. The death of *genre* is what everybody's talking about now. This is plausible, but ultimately not consoling. It's hard to leap to the defense of something as rigid and reactionary and abstract as *genre*. But as used, *genre* is a code word for "the traditional forms and methods of fiction," and those novelists and short story writers willing to accept the death of genre are in effect assenting to an adulteration of the artistic process. They're sacrificing the essential freedom of the creative artist. Distillation, dramatization, distortion, and the other imaginative methods of the creative process are tied to a literalness of no real meaning or necessity. Never before has it been considered appropriate for fiction to be *literally* true. Never before has literary art been bound to actual reality. The true reality of fiction is an *imagined* reality.

Imagination is anyway implicit in the very definition of "fiction," as distinguished from its opposite in the absurd term "nonfiction." And fiction and nonfiction are, again anyway, both perfectly good things in themselves—there doesn't seem to be any *point* in mixing them. The resultant hybrids aren't a new strain of literary art at all. They're just intermittently useful, futureless one-timers, as unaesthetic and recalcitrant as mules.

Real Fiction,
as against the New Fiction

Experimental fiction almost by definition represents a reaction against everything that has been said about the traditional methods of fiction in this book. This is especially true of what is these days called the "New

Fiction" or *nouveau roman* or (perhaps more accurately) "anti-story" or "anti-fiction." A very elaborate rationale has been made about this work, so point-by-point against each of the traditional techniques and effects of traditional fiction as to be virtually a negative-aesthetics.

Thus, the New Fiction proclaims itself to be against plot, against character, against the interaction of plot and character, against meaning, against reality, and so on. The reasons given sometimes seem a bit contradictory to one another, but they all seem to be good enough reasons. Since so few people read fiction anyway these days, it's said, there's no point in writing for readers. Also, the times we live in are too outlandish to be convincingly described in traditional, realistic ways. And, it is said that either this new anti-fiction represents a logical revolution against the literary art which preceded it, or it represents a logical extension of the Modernist movement in literary art which just preceded it.

The New Fiction tries to achieve the "freedom" of modern painting. Like pop art, it is interested in "bad" or "popular" art—in movies, in Superman, Snow White, Lassie, and so on, in advertising, in legendary sports heroes, and in all sorts of other such modern myths and symbols. Like hard-edge painting, the New Fiction conscientiously has no depth, no illusion, no movement. It is often nonrepresentational. It is deliberately static, circular, cyclical, and without development, structure, or event. For something to "happen" in a piece of the New Fiction is like putting something recognizable in an abstract-expressionist painting.

The New Fiction is value-free—against the "traditional" morality of traditional fiction. The New Fiction messes with other media—like graphics and tapes. It often mixes "real" modern history with bizarre imagined events and characters in such a way that it's hard to tell the difference—which is one of the points of it, I guess. It is often close to being "nonfiction," of course. And it is often very "poetic." It goes in just about every conceivable direction in its efforts not to be straight fiction.

The New Fiction is often very interesting—especially in the way it plays with creating illusion and then destroying it deliberately, in its involvement with *how* fiction is made, its interest in the *telling* of the tale, rather than in the tale itself. And, of course, in its humor, especially in its "black humor," it depicts and expresses much about contemporary life.

But the lively tone and method of contemporary literary fiction that *is* fiction must be distinguished from the loony, dull obsessiveness that characterizes much of the experimental writing called New Fiction. One is always being shown excerpts from long, difficult "works-in-progress." So many of these seem conceived in resentment, persisted in with self-defeating young energy or West Coast paranoia, and finally abandoned in bitter realization that no "establishment" publisher will ever take it on. But surely these projects read *better* in excerpt than they would at full length. And surely a lot of them are given up finally not so much because of the hopelessness of publication, but simply because the author himself loses conviction, and perhaps even loses interest, after a while. Even with the shorter pieces of the New Fiction, one is willing for them to end far sooner than they ever usually do. Each new piece may, at the start, impress you with a certain originality of utterance and provoke you by its obliqueness of approach. You wonder what the author is up to, and you can't tell what's going on. But soon, too soon, when you still don't know what's going on, or find out it's not very much, the "originality" of the writing becomes irritating and the obliqueness infuriating. The difficult becomes dull to us as soon as we perceive there's no justification for it. You see that whether this New Fiction is "poetic," or deliberately cliché-ridden, or indented strangely, or doesn't use punctuation or paragraphs, or mixes up chronology, or is printed so that it can be folded into an octagonal form that you can toss back and forth across the *room*, it is, in short, a gimmick, or a combination of gimmicks, that's intrigued you—

innovation used not functionally, as in James Joyce and Samuel Beckett, say, but just to conceal the lack of any story to tell or anything to say. Too often, you feel finally, this difficult, experimental, "innovative" writing represents not the power to go "beyond" traditional fiction form, but rather an attempt to obscure the inability to achieve it. It's minor talents mining out the far-ends of Modernism.

There's always been new *fiction*, by good new young writers. Also, there's always been "new" fiction, backwards and forwards in time from when Djuna Barnes published *Nightwood* (1936). Experimental fiction, let's face it, usually means fiction that really isn't fiction. One sees a lot of novel-length "fiction" manuscripts that aren't novels, and lots of shorter fiction "pieces" or "works" of fiction that aren't short stories. To say, "Oh, boy, we've got a whole 'new' kind of fiction, the idea of it is *nothing happens*," is to deny fiction its own meaning. It's like saying, "We've got this neat new shade of red—*green!*" Why call it fiction at all? Call it something else. "Green writing," say. Or "FAIP," short for Fooling Around In Prose.

Afterword: Writing in General

All of my friends, and most of my acquaintances, are writers of one sort or another, or editors or agents who deal with writers constantly. But it's remarkable how little I know of what happens to writers when they're actually alone writing.

If the way my mind works when I'm trying to write has any resemblance to the way real writers' minds work, then I pity them all. When I have time to write, the ideas aren't there—or if the ideas, then not the words. Forcing myself to put the words on paper helps not at all: insights become platitudes as phrased when writing under self-imposed duress. You *see?!*

If I determine once and for all to finish up a section which has been "nearly finished" for months, then the simplest transitional paragraph evokes related but irrelevant speculations and I find myself furiously scribbling thoughts that get further and further from what I was intending to do, that cover material I know I must some time write, but it's material that I'll want to have make a different point from the point I'm making with it now.

Still, one often stares so blankly for so long at the paper to *no* avail that to be writing anything—and this fast!—is to be exploited while it lasts. And perhaps there are some sentences in it that when later combined with the laborious, correctly directed writing-under-duress can be organized to say what it is that's needed.

Combining them, then, later—determined this time to make a coherent sequence out of all these scraps and all these sets of three or four pages of hasty handwriting, some retyped and some not—I try to construct some sort of bridge between two of these passages, some transitional passage, which somehow gets me started on a related train of thought, but certainly not the one that's needed here, and off I go again, wildly and enthusiastically (but despairingly) scribbling something I hope is good and may have some use later: another disjointed passage to puzzle over.

This is a sample of that.

Can I use it to say that the necessary, planned writing is often the most pedestrian, if not actually awkward, and that what seems most useless when it is being written will often prove not only best but eventually central, because it flows as it comes—which it wouldn't do if it were wrong with the mind, with your own real thoughts on the matter?

But that's not it, not really. Sometimes I can see not only exactly what it was I meant in such-and-such a passage, but also a use for it with a whole new slant. I can comprehend the whole. I can see beyond a few pages to where so-and-so might lead. Befuddlement passes. Superego sneaks away in shame. Energy releases clarity. Clarity releases energy. What paralyzes a writer is the inability to see where what he is writing is going—to see the connections between the aspects of his work. Concentration is all that's needed, really. A deadline releases nervous energy. Adrenalin flows. There's someone who wants the work, is waiting for it. Encouragement's coming, is on the way. No, again that's not it, really. It's more than that. The truth is that the only way not to feel really terrible is to work.

But sometimes it seems easier just to feel really terrible.

Here's a paragraph I scribbled, one that I should have worked in with the passage above, but couldn't. Ideas come complete with words sometimes, but with no relation to the whole conception. The greatest problem is putting all the pieces together. Composed at different times, the passages seem to overlap, often even to contradict, repeat the same examples, sometimes to make one point, sometimes another that's just faintly different. To put them all together into a coherent essay is the problem, and I can stare at the pages for hours, staple them, cut them up, and make no sense of matters at all. My mind is not capable of re-establishing the conviction, much less the emotion, much less the precise rhetoric, with which each was written. The mind is there—it wrote these passages once—why is it gone?

Joyce Carol Oates says she knows the solution to writer's block, and I guess we have to believe she does, considering how much she's written. She says writer's block is caused by some problem in the work that the mind can't consciously solve, and that the solution is to put the work aside for a bit until the subconscious solves the problem.

This solution seems to me to bring up problems of its own. I firmly believe that if you are to get really going in a piece of writing, it has to be what you're concerned about *most* at what point in your life. I mean, sex and carpentry and tennis, say, may all be great recreations from writing, very relaxing, and actually presumably creative for the writing too, if your subconscious is working on those problems that are causing your block because your consciousness can't handle them. But for many of us writers of small conviction and low intensity, the trouble is that even when we're supposed to be working (writing) our subconscious is running over the sex, carpentry, and tennis, or whatever else that, at that point in our lives, *actually* concerns us most.

Some writers do manage, though, really to get into their work sometimes. That it can happen is proved by William Manchester, if by no one else. You remember that Manchester did that big long book on the death of JFK that got him into such a hassle with Jackie and Bobby. At one point, when he was working on it, his editor at Harper's, Evan Thomas, sought him out. Thomas found him in what was described as "a bleak room in a house on the Housatonic River," and apparently the room "contained only three objects, a writing desk, a chair, and a photograph of John F. Kennedy."

That's how you have to strip down if you want to concentrate on what you're doing. It's said that Truman Capote works best in Holiday Inn motel rooms. Anyway, as reported in the New York *World Journal Tribune*, January 29, 1967, Manchester was doing just fine:

> Manchester was writing in longhand. Evidently,
> he had been working long and intensively. There
> was blood on the fingers of his writing hand.

One has to envy this concentration. Of course, at the time, Manchester was sometimes calling his wife "Jackie" and often saying the date was "November 22nd." One envies the ability to work this hard, as one envies any obsessed, near-loony state. We all think it would be nice to be crazy. Certainly it would be easier—as long as one didn't have to work that hard, of course.

Against the way Manchester was working, let me give a sample of my own writing schedule. Say I set out to work just in the morning, start at nine, knock off at 12:30, then do some carpentry or play tennis.

From nine to ten, the struggle is to overcome sense of futility of whole project. Paper shuffling. At ten o'clock decide a start must be made. Typewriter makes first tentative clicks. Awful. Proceed anyway, because just had a thought which ties in with this. At 10:15, begin going good. At 10:30, pause exhausted. There are a million ways this could go, a million things to say, all needed at once to set up what comes next. Got to get it all down. Sudden thirst or need to go to the john, or flies bothering, or hot, or fire going out, getting cold. Never mind, it's going so good now it won't hurt to interrupt for a minute. While drinking water or taking a leak, thinking of project. Yes, it's going good. Potentially a fine book. All this being done now ties in beautifully with that part later that's already done. Must make a note of it. At 10:37, back at desk making note of that part later. Note expands. Never mind, this is good stuff, going great now, would be hard to do later. Working brilliantly. It's 10:45, pause a minute. Exhausted. Does this really fit with the first part? Not the way it's headed, it doesn't. Better leave it, get back to the part I was doing, fix it a bit. Better to take things in order, not skip around too much, get things right as you go. Everything going to fit fine, when you get it straight. Greatest book of its kind in progress here. Now here, where I discuss this, it's too early—I repeat it again later. Ought to have one big wrap-up discussion of this part, all in one place. But no, this is pretty good the way it leads into the other point. Best to leave it the way it is, couldn't really do better than that. But then what about the way the same thing's said later? Jesus, this is a hard business. There really isn't any way to work all these things in together without repeating. Hopeless. What's that noise? What I need is a bleak room on the Housatonic. Thirsty again. Phew, completely let down. Hungry, still an hour to lunch. I ought to be able to work on this later. But then, what about the tennis? Writers need exercise. The trouble is there seems to be only about at most one half hour in any three-hour period devoted to writing in which one is capable of really concentrating and creating. This is usually fifteen minutes on the problem at hand, and fifteen minutes in which one can write well of some more-or-less connected aspect. The solution, for a writer, must be to enlarge those moments if he can, cultivate them, protect them from interruption, from distraction, and try to keep himself on the subject itself. Better jot that down. Oh, this is going to be some book. An honest book. It will really speak to other writers, directly, one writer to another. It'll be great to have it done. Sending it off to be retyped. Don't think of that now. Have to rephrase the dedication, make it more elegant. Then I start daydreaming in earnest, drafting the covering letter to the book editor when I send the manuscript in, writing the reviews and excerpting quotes from them to be used in the advertising, a real professional.

And all afternoon and evening, I feel really terrible.

ABOUT THE AUTHOR

RUST HILLS is generally recognized as having been the best magazine-fiction editor of the 1960s. He has taught the short story at New York University, The New School and Columbia, and is the author of *The Memoirs of a Fussy Man*, a trilogy that is rapidly becoming a humorous classic. He and his wife, the novelist Joy Williams, divide their time between the Florida Gulf Coast and the Connecticut shore.